ACKNOWLEDGMENTS

My thanks to Maureen, her efforts in proofing and endless encouragement have been invaluable.
The excellent 'Resource of Art Quotations' at http://quote.robertgenn.com/ provided most of the quotations.

First Published November 2007

ISBN 978-0-9557586-0-7

Published by Spencer-Bradbury Publishing
Marsh Studio • Hungerford • Berkshire

Printed in the UK by
GoodmanBaylis Worcester
www.goodmanbaylis.co.uk

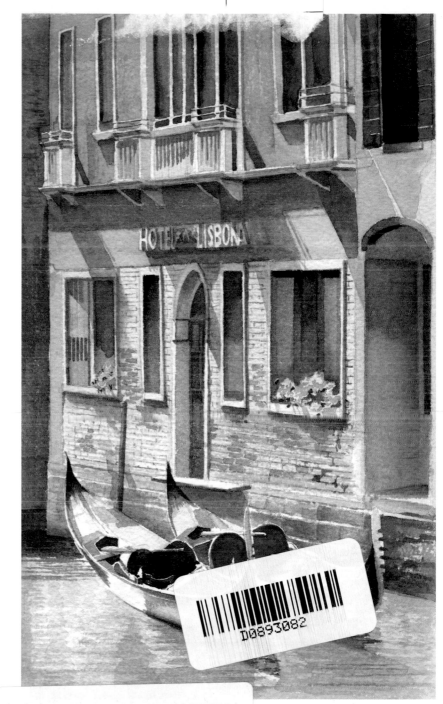

'Gondolas' 2006
Watercolour
11" x 7"

Peter Turner

Painter in oil and watercolour and Illustrator. Peter Turner has lived and painted in Hong Kong, Malaysia, Singapore, Bahrain, France, Germany, and England.

He has exhibited in those countries and taught in France, Germany and England.

Author of the best selling 'PC USER'S GUIDE – Simple Steps to Powerful Personal Computing' published by McGraw-Hill and IBM.

Author and presenter of management training courses and quality workshops.

Art Director and graphics designer for 'e-vision' the quarterly e-commerce magazine.

Tutor for two day painting courses at Marsh Studio Hungerford – www.peterturner.org.

Bunkum – ludicrously false statement, guff, hogwash, rot, bunk, drivel, garbage – a worthless message, bunk – a message that seems to convey no meaning, hokum, meaninglessness, nonsense, nonsensicality, absurdity, absurdness, ridiculousness – a message whose content is at variance with reason, balderdash, fiddle-faddle, piffle – trivial nonsense, buzzword, cant - stock phrases that have become nonsense through endless repetition, cobblers – nonsense; "I think that is a load of cobblers", gibber, gibberish – unintelligible talking, unintelligibility, incoherence, incoherency – nonsense that is simply incoherent and unintelligible, empty talk, empty words, hot air, palaver, rhetoric – loud and confused and empty talk; "mere rhetoric", rigmarole – a set of confused and meaningless statements, hooey, poppycock, stuff and nonsense, stuff – senseless talk; "don't give me that stuff", baloney, bilgewater, boloney, bosh, drool, humbug, tommyrot, tosh, twaddle, tarradiddle – pretentious or silly talk or writing

'There is a lot of Bunkum in the art world, our object is to demystify and encourage more art interested people to paint'

'Painting is a companion with whom one may walk a great part of life's journey' – Sir Winston Churchill.

Essex County Council Libraries

CONTENTS

CONTENTS

Oil and Watercolour Demystified

'if you can write – you can paint'
a Practical Guide

CHAPTER I INTRODUCTION

'If teaching people to paint for the past 45 years has taught me anything, it is that if not exercised, painting abilities will remain dormant and undiscovered for ever. My greatest pleasure is the discovery of these abilities in those who had no idea they existed.'

THE PAINTERS SKILLS

Of the many skills employed in the making of a painting, the painting process itself is the easiest to learn and one which everyone is capable of mastering, *see Figure 4*. In each of these skills everyone has a position on a scale centred on average. In all cases their position on the scale can be improved, in some dramatically with little effort, in others only small changes despite great effort.

Learning to paint – that is mixing and applying the colours – is a 'hand-eye' co-ordination process, like handwriting, riding a bike, driving a car, using chopsticks – everyone can do it. There is no magic, like photographic memory or perfect pitch or drawing ability, which to the frustration of most of us just a few people seem to be born with. Just as when you have learned to write, what you write and in what style, is all important; so having learned to paint what you paint and in what style, becomes the real challenge.

Is it easy to learn? Watercolour is not as easy as the alternatives: Oil, Acrylic, Pastel, Gouache, Water based oils, Water pencils (as many as a creative manufacturing industry can sell to a receptive customer base, seeking – usually in vain – something quicker and easier than traditional oil or watercolour).

Watercolour is different from the others: Beyond a very few seconds before drying, during which time some modification is possible, each stroke is a final commitment. With oil, any

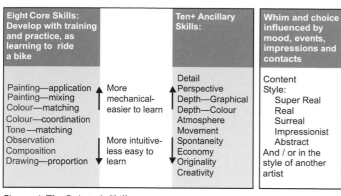

Eight Core Skills: Develop with training and practice, as learning to ride a bike		Ten+ Ancillary Skills:	Whim and choice influenced by mood, events, impressions and contacts
Painting—application Painting—mixing Colour—matching Colour—coordination Tone—matching Observation Composition Drawing—proportion	More mechanical-easier to learn More intuitive-less easy to learn	Detail Perspective Depth—Graphical Depth—Colour Atmosphere Movement Spontaneity Economy Originality Creativity	Content Style: Super Real Real Surreal Impressionist Abstract And / or in the style of another artist

Figure 4. The Painter's Skills

amount of modification (correction) is possible over a period of hours to days. To achieve the required depth of colour or tone with watercolour involves building up layers of 'staining' of the mostly transparent paints, and waiting between layers for the previous applications to dry. For these reasons watercolour imposes itself on the end result to a greater extent than the others. Not, you would imagine, anything to commend it, but there lies its secret, a magical, translucent, fresh, atmospheric, delicate, unique and very desirable end result.

Other aspects of traditional and modern painting also impose themselves on the end result, for example the texture of the painting surface; relative to painting on a smooth wooden panel, does the use of a textured canvas improve an oil painting? Probably not, but it is more practical and arguably longer lasting.

Does the texture applied to the making of watercolour paper improve the end result? The vast majority would say yes. The exceptions include the botanic artists, their choice is still watercolour but without the textured paper – they want nothing to detract from the accuracy and realism of the end result. Then there are the various painting techniques, in oil – a lot of paint versus a little, palette knives in place of brushes, in watercolour – blotting, skimming, scratching, all take part in creating the illusion but are nonetheless visible in the finished painting.

Style

It is fashionable to get 'loose' with watercolour. The intention is to lean toward a more impressionistic, spontaneous, result with the advantage of fast execution. It also reflects

a progression in many famous artists work from graphical toward abstract, however where this exists it usually takes a lifetime of full time painting to accomplish. That this is not a natural progression is also supported by the number of painters who get graphically better as they get older – Salvador Dali, for example. To suggest that a leisure painter should do so regardless of natural style is a backward step in the

Figure 5. 'Crucifixion' (Hypercubic Body) by Salvador Dali – A late Dali graphically better with age © Dali Estate

painter's development. This is also a bias towards a style – not necessarily yours – which should be resisted. In the hands of an accomplished watercolour painter the full range of colour, tone and accuracy is available as in this example from the Scottish artist Henry Brittan Willis – Figure 6. This is about as far as it is possible to get from 'loose' in watercolour and demonstrates the capability of the medium.

All paintings are impressions of the original. The impressions made by watercolour are somehow more evocative, more sensual, and more surreal than the others. In the following examples the 'magic' is we think clear, *see Figures 6-10*. A 'loose' example is included and, as can be seen, in expert hands is very attractive, *see Figure 11*.

For the many who have not drawn or painted for years the initial effort is a voyage of self discovery – how do I rate in each of the skills? And how much effort is necessary to make real progress?

In practice it is difficult for the mechanical processes not to be influenced by a lifetime of likes and dislikes as to style. However, from the word go everyone has their own style – which is to be encouraged, especially at the early stages.

To develop the confidence to produce what you want to produce, as opposed to happy or more often unhappy accidents, the initial efforts should be directed towards accuracy of drawing, tone and colour.

Only when you have learned to use the tools – the results will be by design – and your own style has begun to emerge, should you consider the choice of subject to suit your mood and emerging style. Don't be influenced by others and resist

Figures 7 and 8. 'Blue Boat at Lagos' and 'Green Boat at Lagos' 7" x 10" Manage to capture the character of these Portugese working fishing boats as only watercolour can

the deliberate adjustment of style to reflect that which you admire most in the works of others.

'A picture is first of all a product of the imagination of the artist; it must never be a copy' – Edgar Degas.

The fascination for the tutor is the realisation that we all see colour as differently as line, proportion, tone, composition and perspective, and our application of these skills in painting is infinitely more distinctive and diverse than is our handwriting, which only concerns line.

Just as handwriting is unique and identifiable to an individual so is a drawing or painting, but to a much greater extent. Handwriting is a singular drawing skill. A drawing per se employs skills in proportion, tone, composition, perspective, depth, atmosphere, movement, spontaneity and emotion sufficient to characterise the most demanding of subjects; a painting has all of these plus colour. In addition paintings and drawings may or may not employ originality, creativity, economy (cartooning), exaggeration in line and colour and an overlay of established style including: Super-real, Real, Surreal, Impressionist or Abstract.

'It is a unique and identifiable style which gives a painting its value'

Also the painter's selection of subjects, materials and application techniques all combine to make each work distinct and unique.

This individuality is apparent from the outset and the more works are complete the more distinctive, unique and individualised they become. Hopefully, as in handwriting, this development is involuntary, if it is not it is because influence has been accepted along the way from other artists or worse, critics, an influence that should be resisted – difficult though that is – because good or appealing though it may be, another artists' work is his not your work.

A gallery above all values identifiability, also

Figure 9. Michael Stride's 'Pont Nevern, Pembrokeshire' Watercolour 12" x 16" is a supreme example of observation and interpretation. Watercolour is used here in the best English tradition © Michael Stride

high on the wish list is volume of output, plus subject and style in sympathy with the current fashion (is it commercial). Apart from identifiability these are more influences to be resisted – so long as you do not have to earn your living from painting that is.

What if this natural style is one we may not like? Just as most of us do not change our handwriting because we see one which we like better, to change a painting style for someone else's makes even less sense, especially considering handwriting

is a singular skill whilst painting employs multiple skills.

Leisure paintings should suit the painter, if at the same time they are appealing to others, that is a bonus. If a painter's works consistently enjoy near universal acclaim, this becomes a big incentive; to do more and probably to sell. On the other hand a near universal lack of response is hugely demotivating to many and often the reason they give up and never develop to their full potential. Many are very thankful that L S Lowry did not give up because critics said his drawing was naive. His painting of The Liver Building sold in 2006 for over £1M.

There is a danger here of coming to a premature conclusion about skills and abilities. Like stepping out of a car after 20 minutes of learning and concluding you can't drive, true you can't drive – you haven't learned yet.

Each of the skills mentioned above have to be learned and practised before your potential becomes clear. Do not be put off by any outside influence at least until you are able to draw close to the limit of your ability and get the colour you want in

Figure 10. Brian Walters 'Tracks in the Snow' Postling, Kent 1985. Evocative, atmospheric, a fresh take on an over exposed theme

the places you want it.

As our painting develops we should not succumb to the temptation to paint in the vein of Van-Gogh, Turner, Dali, etcetera, this is not 'you'. First discover what is 'you' then work to make progress in as many of the skills that 'you' regard as valuable. By this process your work will develop more quickly and be more distinctive.

'Whoever the master is whom you prefer, this must only be a directive for you. Otherwise you will never be anything but an imitator' – Paul Cezanne.

It is a unique and identifiable style which gives a painting its value.

WHO NEEDS CRITICISM?

If what you have produced is what you intended, it is beyond criticism.

Unsolicited criticism, is rarely if ever of value, regardless of the source.

Be prepared to ignore it because there is an inbuilt imperative for many people to provide you with the benefit of their criticism whenever they encounter anything that looks

Figure 11. John Yardley R.I. 'Canalside in Venice' Watercolour – the best, in my opinion, of the loose painters – perfect draftsmanship, tone and composition combine to stunning effect © John Yardley

vaguely like art.

If you ask for criticism in an effort to improve mechanical issues, that is a very different proposition and can be of significant value.

This point is made to stress that your work is 'you'; to modify it at the whim of someone else is invariably a backwards step in your development.

Everyone can write – everyone can paint. This is rich and fertile ground with something in it for everyone. If a change is as good as a rest, painting is the rest you need and the sooner you start the more will be your pleasure and reward.

SUBJECTS

In a world where an unmade bed is said to be art—you could start with abstract painting, but it is not recommended. Learning to mix and apply the paint without a reference would be like learning to drive in a field or to wind surf with no wind.

Unless you have a photographic memory, and that is very rare (current research suggests it does not exist),

everything you paint will need a reference.

There is a strict order for the source of your reference: First, and well above the rest, is 'from life'. You select the subject, composition, lighting; you convert from three dimensions, in short it is entirely your creation.

Next is 'a photograph which you have taken with a view to painting', often the only practical solution and much more efficient than yesteryears sketch book. The downside with using photographs is the lack of practise in converting three dimensions to two and as their initial choice is influenced by good composition, the practise in composition and the opportunities to improve the picture can get overlooked. Then, well down, comes 'someone else's photo'. There are copyright issues and it is not going to be your picture. Last, a long, long way behind even someone else's photo comes 'someone else's painting'. You will learn nothing about the subject, its composition, tone and style that looking at it will not teach you and since you were not there when the painting was made you will probably have no knowledge of the materials used or the techniques applied. Your own style will be compromised and your aim at an identifiable style and subject set will be at best confused, be inspired by other painter's but don't copy them.

'Don't be a blueprint. Be an original' – Roy Acuff.

With the advent of www.flickr.com there is a wealth of valuable photo reference material available to all. However, if you intend to sell a painting based on a photo with a declared copyright, take care to check with the owner of the copyright first. If there is no copyright, the danger exists that other artists may use the same reference – not so much a legal problem as an embarrassing one. This is not as academic as it may sound because among the many thousands of photos, there is just a handful which make good paintings* and a real possibility that someone else will agree with you.

*You will doubtless discover this when searching among your many photos for reference material.

Learning to draw and paint is a hurdle which we need to get past before the real challenges begin. Paint, paper, canvas, etc. are tools which, like a pen and writing paper or a piano, we need to learn how to use before we can move on. No short-cut has ever improved the end result, whether we are learning a language, or to drive, draw, paint, play a musical instrument, or any other skill.

There is skill in making a bed but no skills are needed to produce an unmade bed.

Subjects Check List (content)

Animals, Architectural – street scenes – buildings – cityscapes – interiors, Birds, Botanical illustration – plants
Fantasy, Genre (everyday life), Historical, Landscape – trees – skies – water – mountains – rivers – canals – locks – bridges – reflections, Mythology, Non-Objective
People – portrait – figures – life studies – groups – children Political, Religious, Seascape – beach scenes – harbours – boats, Sport, Still life – flowers – fruit – veg. – food – drink – wine, Story.

'Beauty is everywhere, but one may see the beautiful view and the other sees a dirty window. You have the power within you to choose what you see, what you think and what you paint' – Leanne Cadden.

'The love of beauty in its multiple forms is the noblest gift of the human cerebrum' – Alexis Carrel.

'You can't fake quality (in art) any more than you can fake a good meal' – William S. Burroughs.

Drawing
seeing is believing?

CHAPTER II DRAWING

The difference between one who can Draw and one who can't is the ability to see what is wrong – with the line, its length, angle, relationship with other lines with ellipses at wrong angles, with horizons that slope and churches that lean to name but a few. There are classic lapses in drawing in many famous paintings from artists you would expect should know better. Years after being professor of perspective at the Royal Academy WMJ Turner's church's were often leaning to the left. And Caravaggio's gaffs are inexplicable from one with such an amazing grasp of reality, *see Figure 12.*

It is not difficult to check for these very common problems.

Any mechanical help to see what is wrong will improve the drawing.

Use a rule or Tee Square. Draw centre lines through symmetrical objects and all ellipses. Look at the drawing upside down or better, in a mirror – an indispensable tool especially for portraits. Constantly check lengths, angles and relationships and if all else fails ask one who, with a fresh view, can see the problems. The longer you work on a drawing the easier it is to drift into being deceived.

Construction lines

—improve everyone's ability to avoid leaning buildings, ellipses and horizons. They are nearly essential to an acceptable reproduction of a symmetrical object such as a jug or glass. Always draw the complete ellipse about its centre line, even if you only need half of it, and note that the lower ellipse is deeper not flatter than those above it. We know the base is flat and so tend to flatten objects which stand on a surface.

The drawing which precedes a painting is very different from a drawing in its own right. The natural habits to sketch and to use a lot of lead are both ruinous in paintings. The ideal is a just discernible single line. The ideal pencil is the popular .5mm clutch pencil, its fine HB lead is near

Figure 12. Caravaggio ('Bacchus' 1596 Galeria Uffizi) had a problem with ellipses. The base of the glass leans down to the left as does the wine in the carafe.
With apologies to a much admired work.
Had the picture been finished things may have been different

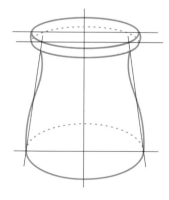

Right – Multi pencil with smudging, others 2b only and no smudging

perfect and messy sharpening is avoided.

Because lead of any amount does take the edge off light tones, some artists 'draw' with a brush and a thin wash of colour selected not to interfere with the final painting, but these strokes are not as easy to erase or change as pencil so the object of the accurate guide and corrected composition are compromised.

Do not forget to remove the construction lines, especially prior to watercolour painting. As soon as even a thin wash covers a pencil line, it becomes difficult or impossible to erase, because some of the glue size also covers the line.

With oil painting, do not erase near the palette – it is a disaster if those 'bits' get into the paint. An alternative is to use a putty rubber – no 'bits' but not as effective as an eraser.

Drawing as a Drawing

To achieve the full tonal depth in a drawing, a soft (2b or 3b) pencil is needed for the shading. All of the planning and compositional work is the same as a painting – fine, just visible lines, which can easily be moved, until all of the elements are in the correct place. Now instead of painting we finish the picture with shading – from white paper to solid black.

In my early drawings, many different pencils were employed, from 2h to 6b, plus smudging and erasing. Gradually over the years, except for a single 2b used on a hot pressed (smooth) watercolour paper, all have fallen by the wayside.

Smudging does little to better characterise the subjects,

plus it stands out and looks unnatural.

This is one person's conclusion which should not influence you. Your decisions should come after experimenting and a great deal of practise.

Sharpening

—is an unavoidable pain, in which you need to develop some skill, because much of the shading is achieved by employing the side of the lead as opposed to the point. If you work in this way the grain in the paper is critical and you will need to search and practise to find the optimum pencil and paper combination to suit your style.

Tone

Depth is lost in the process of translating three dimensions to two, so try from the outset to achieve at least as much tone and contrast as is in the reference.

Unwanted Smudging

Beware; it is very easy to smudge a drawing, especially in transit. Clamp backing and protection pages either side of the drawing, so that they cannot move, using large bulldog clips. When returning from Hong Kong, without following this advice, the Chinese boys on the previous page, which were drawn without smudging, were all but ruined.

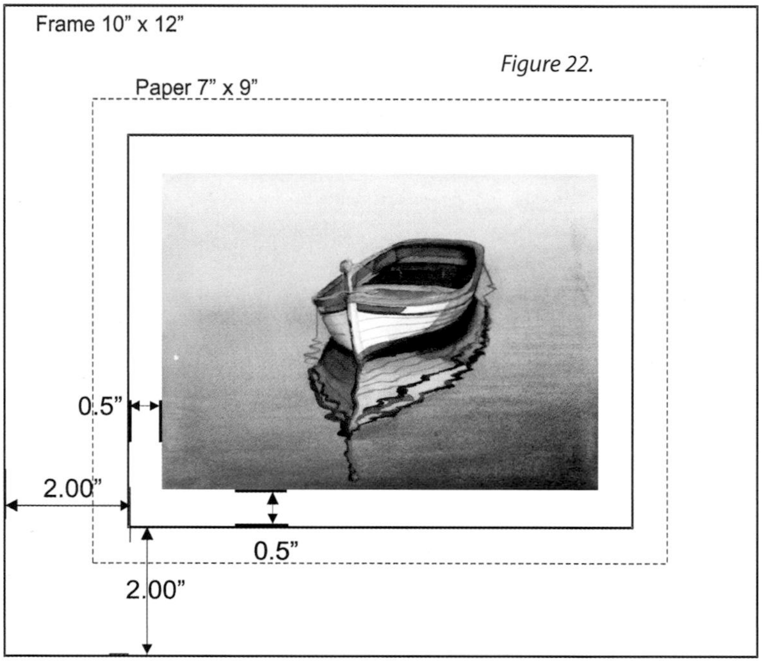

COMPOSITION

Anything done to improve the composition will improve the painting. Obvious – maybe but it needs to be said. Composition doesn't 'emerge' during the course of a painting and contrary to popular practise it is not resolved by cropping the final work. It needs to be carefully planned.

Here are some of the aspects to be considered: Line, colour

and tone composition each have a critical impact on the final composition. To slavishly follow a reference from life or photo is to miss valuable opportunities to 'improve' many aspects of the picture, especially its composition.

Skies and backgrounds at the moment of drawing or taking a photo are rarely the most appropriate for the foreground subject. Simplification, emphasis, de-emphasis, colour and tonal changes can 'improve' the composition, its impact and / or the impression of depth, atmosphere, movement, emotion and spontaneity.

For several years now half an inch or so of clear space has surrounded each watercolour. The painting stops at a pre-drawn frame, *see Figure 22*. In addition to resolving how and where to sign on dark and light paintings, easing the signing of limited edition prints, ensuring that the painting will perfectly fit into a standard frame, and looking good,

the main reason is to force consideration of the composition from the outset,

and hopefully get it right first time – as in an oil where cropping is not a practical option.

There are no unbreakable rules for composition but there are guidelines and tips established over centuries which are unwise to ignore. Shadows help provide a base to objects which would otherwise seem to 'float'. Strong shadows which tend to lead the eye off the picture disturb its harmony and distract from the subject. A portrait should have at least as much below the chin as above, to provide a base and prevent the head from seeming to float. The ideal size for a portrait is a little smaller than life size. More space above than below a subject improves the composition.

More subjective but still well founded points include:

Frame 10" x 12"

Paper 7" x 9"

Figure 22.

0.5"

2.00"

0.5"

2.00"

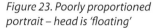

Figure 23. Poorly proportioned portrait – head is 'floating'

Better proportioned portrait – as much below the chin as above

Attracting the eye toward the main subject. Not detracting from the main subject with too much content and / or colour in the background or adjacent objects. Avoiding conflicting angles. Balancing angles and strong objects.

Composition like drawing and all of the other skills needs to be practised. It is easy to practise 'painting' from photos and to accept the total photo as a composed picture but this is a mistake; you are not developing your skills in composition. Ideally 'compose' every picture, including all of the practise ones. Look at every photo reference with a viewing frame. Decide what should be the centre of attention, 'frame' it – zoom in and out, then compose it, add or remove irrelevant clutter, do a trial sketch or two – better – use photo-editing.

Be sure all the changes are improvements.

Of the faults that are found after the completion of a work, compositional errors are probably the most common and often very elusive, sometimes taking years to appreciate. The message is the same, all of the skills need to be learned and practised.

Emphasis in Composition

—the impact in many of the most famous images has been produced by emphasis of selected items and de-emphasis of others often by 'exaggerating' tone, colour and content. Caravaggio may not have invented it but certainly made the absolute most of it especially in his day of prescriptive control of everything religious.

His depiction of Christ in 'The Supper at Emmaus' © *National Gallery, London.* was branded heretical by many at the time, not least by dressing everyone in the costume of the day (1601) and using 'realism' to depict Christ.

Rubens also employed this dramatic emphasis as in 'Christ's Charge to Peter' c 1616 *Reproduced by permission of the Trustees of the Wallace Collection, London.* and 'Two Satyrs', © *Bridgeman Art Library / Alte Pinakothek, Munich* – Joseph Wright some 150 years later employed similar emphasis in his 'An Experiment on a Bird in the Air Pump' 1768 © *National Gallery, London.* Note: Spotlights had yet to be invented.

'Imagination rules the world' (Napoleon)

PILOT COMPOSITIONS

Most of these are 'Wise after the event' amendments –

the real challenge is to get the composition correct before painting is started.

Because we are not good at visualising the effect of changes 'Pilot' tone drawings or complete paintings are often necessary if an 'error' in composition is to be avoided.

When working from photographs, these pilots can most easily be done by photo-editing, *see page 32*. The Camera's Place in Art.

Note: Some of these changes are more subjective then others.

Left – Too much space right of door, pot is afterthought

Right – Pot better integrated

Left – Hard shadow leads eye off the picture – disturbing the harmony
Right – Harmony restored

Left – Shadow faded but not enough
Right – Improved

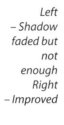  

Left – Too much space above and to the right
Right – Harmony restored – the most subjective in this small group

Left – Too central and not enough space above
Right – Improved

Too much blue sky above and to the right

Not improved by cropping

Surprise—dramatic sky does nothing for the picture

Blue solved and surreal sky complements the photo

1. Move the fruit to the left – improves the composition
2. How far is the pot vertical centre from the canvas centre
3. Mark the top of the pot anchor point
4. Mark the bottom of the pot anchor point
5. Mark the bottom of the fruit's shadow

Anchor Point

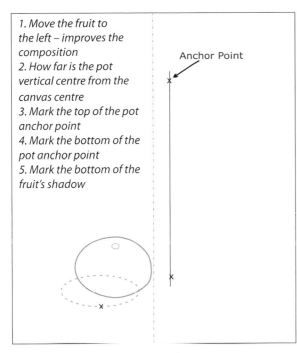

DRAWING FROM A REFERENCE

A single just visible fine line is needed, to achieve this, some will have to break their 'sketching' habit. Compose in a viewing frame – position the key elements and adjust the Zoom. Look for where in the reference the horizontal and vertical centres of the composition are to be.

9. Only when correct, draw spout and handle, otherwise they will throw your eye off.
10. Complete drawing and remove construction lines – is the composition too far to the right?

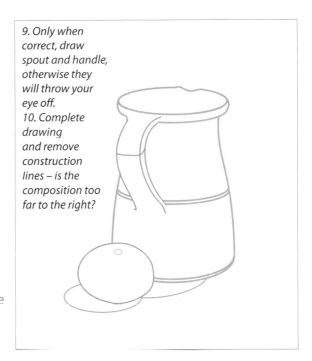

6. Complete centre lines for the ellipses
7. Draw complete ellipses
8. Erase and redraw, probably several times to get positions and proportions correct

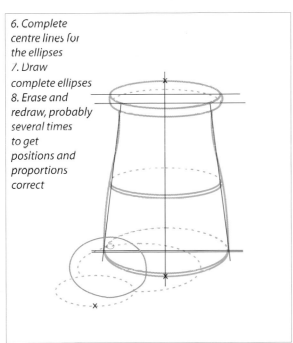

PROPORTION

Getting things in proportion is one of the most demanding of the needed skills. We have previously highlighted the improvement available if construction lines are used.

There are many other aids that can be employed.

Measurement

—tools can include: dividers, tee squares, protractors and rulers to make length and angle measurements and comparisons. It is probably going too far to suggest the use of an epidiascope or camera obscura.

On the other hand, 'squaring up' is considered valid, especially when a large change in scale is involved. By looking at the picture upside-down or in a mirror we can often see elements which have drifted out of proportion during the drawing process.

The process of drawing in proportion is to observe and replicate similar heights, lengths and angles

Squaring Up

—is a technique to transfer, usually a two dimensional drawing or photo to a new surface. A grid is drawn on the original or on a transparent sheet which is placed over the original. The grid is then reproduced often on a larger scale on the new picture and the content of each square copied from the original to the new picture. It is a very effective way of preserving proportions in particular of faces and figures.

It has been used in the past by artists to copy or scale a work smaller or larger, sometimes much larger, which could also be completed by a team of other painters, very large murals for example.

The technique has been used on live subjects by employing a device called a Drawing Frame.

In 1525 the artist Albrecht Dürer published a series of illustrations of drawing frames and perspective machines and John Constable occasionally used a glass frame to transfer from life to a painting. A drawing frame is a grid between the artist's eye and the subject.

Drawing for watercolour.

The way most of us draw 'in proportion' is similar to squaring up but does not involve squares as such. What we look for are 'anchor points' – the Xs above, we make numerous comparisons and measurements increasing the anchor points until we are satisfied that the overall structure is sufficiently characterised and in good proportion. The process includes searching for similar measurements and angles throughout the picture. Each of the green lines are of equal width. The small violet lines are of equal height. The yellow lines are either horizontal or vertical and help in the comparison process. The more we look the more we are likely to find. A rule, or dividers are usually the means of making the measurements or comparisons. This in turn is virtually the same process as when people hold a pencil at arms length and compare measurements and angles at various points in a 'from life' situation.

When life is not the best reference

It is not unusual to encounter elements in a reference, from life or a photo, which if painted would not look right. The sea going up and down hill is a case in point, see the reference photo. In the painting the sea has been 'straightened'.

How often have we said or heard this: 'Isn't that beautiful, it doesn't look real does it?'

Beautiful it may be but probably it will not look real or good in a painting so the best policy is to modify or avoid it.

The Reference

The Painting

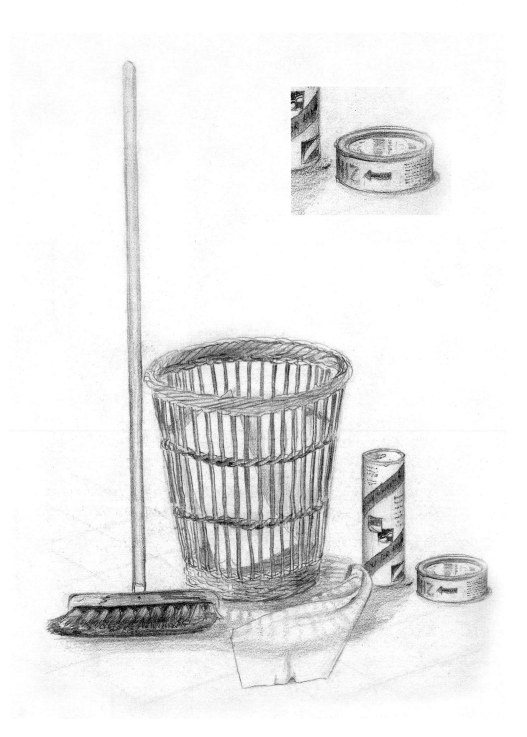

Study for an A Level examination 1957 – 2B pencil – from life using materials at hand to reference the drawing of various objects and textures

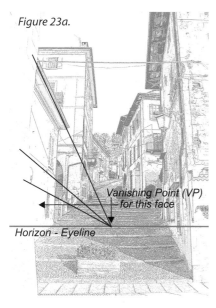

Figure 23a.

Vanishing Point (VP)
for this face

Horizon - Eyeline

PERSPECTIVE

Perspective is about geometry, precision, and rules. Not naturally high in many artists priorities. Without them however, many a fine work of art has been diminished.

As with drawing, aids to see what is wrong, are essential tools.

The basic rules are not difficult but their application in some circumstances can be complicated.

Relative to the subject the viewer can be above, level, or below but also at a distance (as in a telephoto – little perspective) or close (as in a wide-angle photo – a lot of perspective). Positioning yourself is as important as 'framing' the picture. Framing is how much will be included, (zooming) and with what aspect ratio.

The level at which the eye is viewing the scene is known as the eyeline (also the horizon). At this line there are no perspective angles. To establish the eyeline in a street scene where there may be little or no obvious lines at eye level, you would select perhaps a gutter line and a down stairs windowsill line and extend them until they cross. This crossing establishes both the eyeline and the vanishing point (VP) for that face of the building, *see Figure 23a*. If the street were curving to the left the VP for the building next further away would be more to the left, but still at the eyeline. In this case the street curves to the left then to the right. Note the much higher building Bldg. 2 obeys the same rules.

Also note the vertical eyeline, for which the VP in this case is above the horizontal eyeline, this is because the flagstones are inclined upwards toward the steep hill. For a flat surface it would meet at the horizontal eyeline. Note also that the same rules apply to roofs or balconies which overhang the walls, recessed or protruding they are all in the same plane and so will conform exactly to the rules.

When drawing a complex scene such as this it is very easy to get some of the many angles wrong. Using these simple rules, each surface and its associated VP and angles, can be easily checked.

Vertical perspective

—in a painting or studio photograph the vertical perspective is usually removed, because the eye / brain, when presented

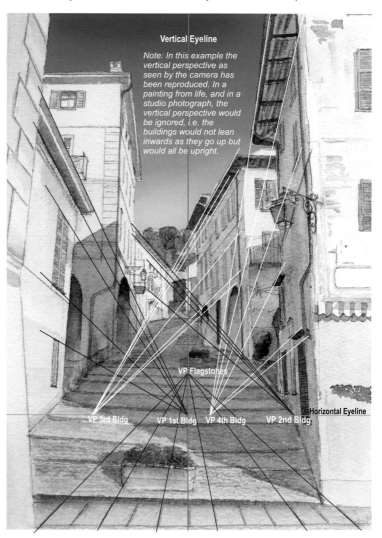

Vertical Eyeline

Note: In this example the vertical perspective as seen by the camera has been reproduced. In a painting from life, and in a studio photograph, the vertical perspective would be ignored, i.e. the buildings would not lean inwards as they go up but would all be upright.

VP Flagstones

Horizontal Eyeline

VP 3rd Bldg   VP 1st Bldg   VP 4th Bldg   VP 2nd Bldg

with a two dimensional picture, cannot cope with glasses or buildings that lean. Another reason why a photographic reference should not be accepted without 'improving' its content and composition.

Whilst we are happy to accept in *Figure 52a* the table mat's vertical perspective, because we know it is flat on the table, when reproducing this as a painting we would make the glass upright as in *Figure 52b*. In this case the solution is not photo-

Figure 52a. As seen sat at the table c 24" from the glass, the 'real' view. To achieve this a wide angle lens is needed

Figure 52b. 'Corrected' for vertical perspective to make the glass stand upright, 'because we know glasses cannot lean'

Figure 53a. Original reference photograph. The camera sees what we see but we can't live with that. This is the town of Orta by lake Orta in northern Italy. A steep hill, a winding street and a lot of perspective both horizontal and vertical, make this a challenge

Figure 53b. 'Corrected' for vertical perspective to make the buildings stand upright, because 'we know buildings do not lean'. Note: This is a photo-edited version of Figure 14a with vertical perspective and barrel distortion removed, lighting adjusted and the ugly cable banished

editing but taking the shot from approximately six feet from the glass, i.e. not wide angle.

Note: The mat now looks even more 'right'. In effect we are changing reality because wide angle reality, when converted into two dimensions 'does not look right'.

Figure 53b is what should have been used as the reference for the painting on the previous page.

The remarkable fact is that because the centre of our narrow focus is always upright, when painting this scene from life, virtually all of us would remove the vertical perspective without giving any of what is written here a single thought.

Horizontal perspective must be obeyed, vertical not...

Street scenes and interiors have many perspective issues. In a photo of a street scene, where people are walking, many of them will not make good painting subjects. When frozen by a camera more than half of the shots of a walking person will look 'unnatural' and will require substitutes. Adding an element to a picture is much more difficult than taking one away. Size, lighting, perspective, appropriate clothes, all need to be 'right'.

In *Figure 54*. A new person is added at point X. Because all of the people's heights are related to their positions and are projections to the eyeline, connecting the feet to the eyeline to find the VP then from the VP to the Head of the reference person R. the height of the new person can be accurately determined. The same of all items that are the same height.

Note: Everything in the picture has a new perspective when the viewer moves, the feet waist lines, eyes – everything.

As in the first example on perspective, we are not using anything new, just an eyeline, projections and VPs, simple tools to get things right.

If instead of one hut there were several, equally spaced, finding out the correct depth for the next hut is not a case of scaling the height and width. For this we need to understand foreshortening.

From this point things get progressively more complicated, it is well to remember that what follows is needed to construct a perspective drawing without a reference, something few of us will ever do. We include it here to help understand the principles.

Foreshortening

—is not quite so simple. The current view of the hut shows less width on the shaded side than the front. If the viewer

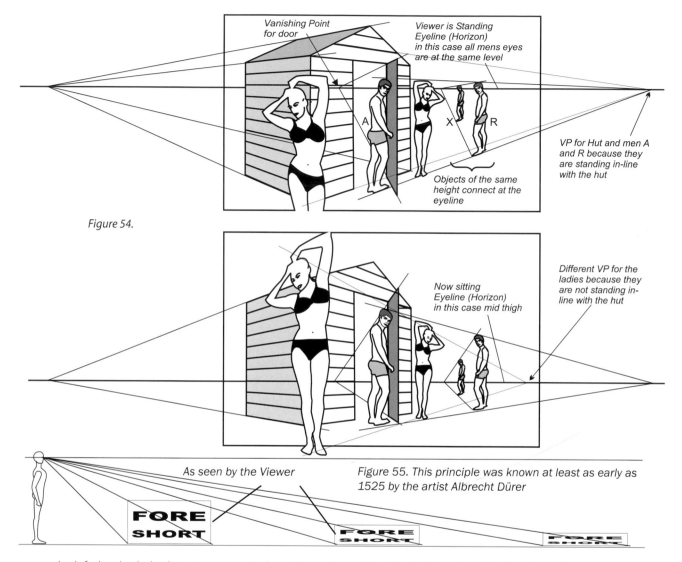

Figure 54.

Vanishing Point for door

Viewer is Standing
Eyeline (Horizon)
in this case all mens eyes
are at the same level

VP for Hut and men A
and R because they
are standing in-line
with the hut

Objects of the same
height connect at the
eyeline

Now sitting
Eyeline (Horizon)
in this case mid thigh

Different VP for the
ladies because they
are not standing in-
line with the hut

As seen by the Viewer

Figure 55. This principle was known at least as early as
1525 by the artist Albrecht Dürer

FORE
SHORT

FORE
SHORT

FORE
SHORT

moves to the left the shaded side gets progressively wider and the front narrower.

Estimating these widths for a given viewing position is getting the 'foreshortening' correct. The degree of foreshortening is determined once again from an eyeline and a VP. In *Figure 55*. a six foot square sign is placed at three distances from the viewer. In as little as 35 feet, the sign is hardly readable. Placed half a mile away the height of the sign is so thin as to be invisible. It is the ratio of viewer height to distance from the object that determines the foreshortening.

Using the same principle we can establish the foreshortening of, for example, a tiled floor, fence posts, lamp posts or a paved area. Waves in the sea half way to the horizon (three to four miles) should be less than a hairline if a tsunami is to be avoided.

OBSERVATION

Applied to drawing—If asked to draw an eye from memory, i.e. no reference or mirror, the result for most of us will be as

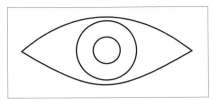

Figure 56.

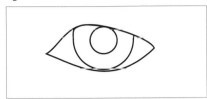

Same number of lines – better observed

Eyelids are part of and characterise the eye

Some shading...

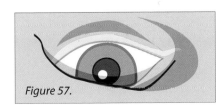

Figure 57.

Figure 56. There is no sense that this is a left or right eye or if it upside-down or not. It may be attractive because it is different and it is saying this is an eye, but the viewer is disconcerted because it is clearly 'wrong'. It does not have to be complicated to dispel this tension, as the cartoonists ably confirm, but the characteristics which describe an eye do need to be there.

Although we look at eyes most days of our lives we do not keep a memory of their structure or proportions, nor do we for a face, figure, cat, car, house, etc. To create a representation which is not going to disconcert the viewer we all need a reference – from life or a photo. This is not an issue of observation but of memory and our memory for graphical objects is very short. An object in front of us is one thing but place the object in another room, just a few seconds away and our ability to characterise it is hugely impaired.

In *Figure 57*, we see the same eye upside-down. The reason that it looks so alien is because we rarely see it that way. In this case it is the shading of the eye that is critical. Most light comes from above and the eye itself is shaded by the eyebrow and the eyelid. If the shading above the eye is removed it will invariably look wrong.

It is reasonable to conclude that in creating an impression avoiding distraction, the key elements need to be characterised and in a form that is most often seen. As in writing, the better the description the better the communication. Anything included that is clearly 'wrong' will distract, disconcert and cloud the communication, often to a disproportionate degree; an eye higher or larger than it should be, a horizon which is not flat, one side of a symmetrical object which is different from the other, a wrong perspective or colour, and so on.

This is not to say that distraction in itself has no place in art. When used to stir the emotions as in L S Lowry, John Bellany or Picasso, the artists have deliberately contrived to evoke an emotional response which distracts and disconcerts – but this is a subject for another time.

Getting your eye in

—as it is often called – is really a process of refreshing the brain's memory with an object's structure, proportions, colour and tone.

Ask a full time portrait artist to draw a face without a sitter and the result would be impressive. Ask the same artist to draw a monkey without a reference and the result would be poor.

This particular brain has a good medium term memory of the characteristics which describe a human face but, like the rest of us, no memory or practise of a monkey.

Having drawn several monkeys from life or photos – now the monkey can be drawn convincingly without a reference.

What you see not what you know

We know a tree is green and has many branches but this is not true when viewing from a distance, the green is more a grey blue and the branches are a blur. In many cases there is a need to look long and hard to identify what you are really seeing and substitute it for what you know – more so from life than a photograph. What colours to paint in the background of *Figure 58*, is much more difficult than it looks and a too detailed drawing will often lead to an over worked painting.

Regardless of how observant you are, taking up drawing and painting adds a new level of observation.

Some tutors talk about 'teaching students how to see'. This is too brutal, no one likes to think that they cannot see. Practise

Grey blue

Black?

Figure 58. Not all shadows are equal...

however, and quite a lot of it , is needed if you are not to miss opportunities to better characterise and describe a subject.

'A heightened sense of the observation of nature is one of the chief delights that have come to me through trying to paint' – Sir Winston Churchill.

'The faculty of creating is never given to us all by itself. It always goes hand in hand with the gift of observation' – Igor Stravinsky.

Practise makes Perfect

When we draw from life we are practising all of the skills except colour. In a drawing we use composition, perspective, proportion, creativity, artistic license., conversion from three to two dimensions and if we go on to shade the drawing then we add tone, contrast, modelling, etc.

The drawing may take less time than the painting but it is 90% of the picture, its composition and creativity.

At all stages of our development we can never do too much drawing. Draw wherever you are whenever you con.

Draw wherever and whenever you can

Colour Theory and Painting Practice

'The Case for a Limited Palette'

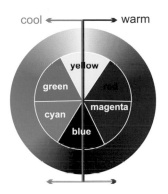

cool ←——————→ warm

yellow
green
red
cyan
magenta
blue

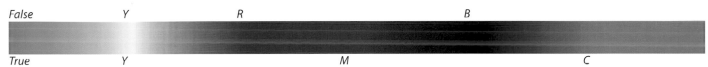

False   Y   R   B

True   Y   M   C

What were falsely assumed to be the paint primaries were quite a long way from the true primaries.

CHAPTER III COLOUR

We join here a lively and crowded debate which has raged since painting began. Our contribution is to provide a practical summary of the theories and approaches to colour reproduction and to keep abreast of today's paint technology.

For several hundred years artists have struggled to make primary colours work. It isn't that they didn't know of their existence, the problem has been that two of their chosen three were incorrect, leading to unsatisfactory results. All of the pictures in all of the glossy magazines, including this book, are produced from the three primary colours, cyan, magenta and yellow plus black. Gainsborough's 'Blue

Gainsborough's 'Blue Boy' was painted with just three pigments
Courtesy of the Huntington Library, Art Collections, and Botanical Gardens, San Marino, California

Boy' was painted with just three pigments. Why then do the makers offer dozens of colours?

The most obvious answer is that they are in the business of selling paints – each maker has a 'Recommended palette', occasionally published more often determined by its choice in 'sets' 10 to 12 or more colours, one talks of 36 essential colours.

Unfortunately for the painter there is no clear consensus between makers. Not to be too cynical, artists also have themselves to blame. Most artists have a favourite palette and irrefutable arguments as to why each colour is indispensable, but again, a consensus is hard to find.

The fact is that paints have personalities and like personalities we come to like and dislike them. More or less transparency, opacity, saturation and permanence. High and low staining ability, watercolours that do or do not granulate. Some are old friends despite their delinquent habits, others have romantic names, even more are sold following a rave review from a respected artist. In their search for individualism it is not difficult to convince the majority of artists to be non-conformist, so why follow a consensus – supposing there was one?

There are aspects of practicality in the execution of art which are not clever to ignore. One of paintings great frustrations is arriving at a colour and not remembering how you got there. The more colours you start with the greater is the frustration. Most professional artists 'eventually' settle for a limited palette often having experimented with everything available in the belief that otherwise they may 'miss out'.

What soon becomes clear is that despite painting full time no one can remember the huge number of combinations even a small palette demands. In a palette consisting of just the three primaries plus black and white, there are over a million combinations that the eye is capable of discerning. Add one more colour and the number is 100 million. So we settle for the maximum coverage of the colours with the minimum number of paints. In theory and in the practical examples of commercial printing, that is the three primaries Cyan, Magenta and Yellow plus Black and White (white paper in watercolour and commercial printing). In practice the closest we can get to genuine primaries varies with manufacturer. The Italian maker Maimeri includes 'Primary Yellow', 'Primary Blue – Cyan', and 'Primary Red – Magenta' in its artists watercolours and oils (available from jacksonsart.co.uk).

Winsor and Newton's recommendation is as close as makes little practical difference: Winsor Blue (Green shade), Permanent Rose and Winsor Yellow – Winsor and Newton say Lemon Yellow but in practice we have found Winsor yellow to be more capable.

Cyan (a greenish blue) Magenta (a bluish red) and Yellow are not an accidental or arbitrary choice but dictated by the science of colour or to be more precise the human response to colour.

Our eyes detect colour using three, Red, Green and Blue sensors, called Cones. They detect the proportion of each of the three coloured lights that they see and report back to the brain. They have the remarkable ability to differentiate between millions of colours and shades.

An object, e.g. a leaf, or a paint has the ability to absorb all colour except the one we see. When illuminated with white light, for example sunlight, which is the addition of all colours, only a narrow portion of the full spectrum is seen and becomes an object with a given colour; green in this example. Because paint primaries work by subtractive mixing but light primaries (RGB) by additive, the equivalents of the RGB for paint have to be inverted, *see Figure 62*. The complementary colour to Blue (Blue inverted) is Yellow. Red becomes Cyan and Green Magenta. The main characteristics of paint primaries are:

It is not possible to mix a primary from other primaries.

The three colours capable of making the maximum number of other colours.

All three (CMY) mixed will equal black (when the light primaries, R,G and B, are added the result is white).

To achieve the full range of tones for each primary and save on the cost of using expensive CMY for blacks, printers also add Black (which when used in smaller and smaller percentages – through all the tones of grey – ends up as white, i.e. no ink, just white paper). This set of four inks is known as CMYK. Back to paint – the RGB colours can be achieved in paint by mixing each of the ink/dye/paint primaries with its neighbour: magenta and yellow = red, yellow and cyan = green and cyan and magenta = blue. Now we have 6 paints and a corrected version of the traditional artists colour wheel. – *see Figure 63*, NEW.

All the remaining millions of colours that the trio is capable of producing and the eye capable of determining are achieved by mixing various combinations and amounts of the 3 primaries plus black and white. The key point is, even though this is c 50% of the colours the eye is capable of discerning – *see Figure 65*, the eye is only capable of achieving this amazing feat when each variation is side by side and contain only pure tones. In practice in life, or a photo, variations do not lay next to each other and are a mass of colour and tone variations. The

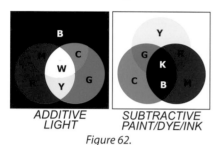

ADDITIVE LIGHT   SUBTRACTIVE PAINT/DYE/INK
Figure 62.

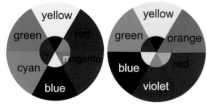

Figure 63. New and Old Artist's Colour Wheels. In 1671 Newton suspected that the primaries were RGB and CMY but it took until the 19th century to prove it. Amazingly many text books still use the incorrect Old version with the primaries as yellow, red and blue. See Appendix C for a more complete artists colour wheel.

The centre circle is inverted and shows the true complements in the New wheel and the erroneous ones in the Old wheel.

100% Yellow	100% Yellow + 4% Magenta
100% Cyan	100% Cyan + 2% Red
100% Magenta	100% Magenta + 4% Cyan

Figure 65. Small variations in adjacent tones can be perceived

The same variation over 7 steps

16,000,000 colours

256 colours

16 colours

Figure 66. No difference between 250 and 16 Million?

only near pure tones that exist are generated by computer graphics. It is clear that, for practical purposes, the colours that are missing from the primary Ink/paint set are only perceivable under unnatural conditions.

How do we find out how many colours are needed to render an accurate picture? In the example spectra – *see Figure 66*, clearly 16 is not enough but no difference seems apparent between 250 and 16 Million, when the photos are enlarged however, we see that they are not the same – notice the leaves in *Figure 67c*, the colours are separated as in a contour map. This demonstrates that 250 is not good enough for quality photography. To render a scene from life, 5,000 (0.5% of the

eye's capability) is plenty and those that are missing from the several million at our disposal will never be seen.

Before we move on we need to talk about saturation, also known as colour purity and Chroma. Chroma is a way of measuring saturation. Saturation is the amount of colour, relative to black or white, which exists in a paint, i.e. Black and White are unsaturated, the absence of black or white in a colour results in its maximum saturation. Theory determines that mixing two primaries of maximum saturation results in a secondary with 2/3 of maximum saturation. In practice however most colours in life are not even close to maximum saturation.

If there is a problem with green in a landscape it is usually that the painter has used over saturated colours (too much colour), even if produced from Yellow and Blue. Yes you can buy Winsor Green Yellow Shade PG36 and get a more saturated green, and you may need to because it is a favourite for many manufactured products, but if used in a landscape it will stand out to such an extent that it will ruin the picture.

On the rare occasions that you do need near fully saturated colours, make use of the non primaries but only on a case by case basis.

If less than fully saturated colours were a problem, every photo in every magazine would look dull and if artists were able to achieve the colour accuracy of commercial printing their ability to achieve the colours they wanted would be greatly increased.

Figure 67a. 256 colours

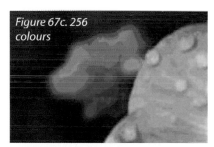

Figure 67c. 256 colours

Figure 67b. 16,000,000 colours

Figure 67d. 16,000,000 colours

For those who are not interested in accuracy either of colour, tone or saturation, and many painters achieve some startling effects and interesting results by ignoring reality, *see Figure 68*, then yes, in addition to the green above, buy Winsor Orange Red Shade PO73 and Ultramarine Violet PV15– you now have 100s of million choices with many closer to maximum saturation – *see Figure 69*, and note that the reproduction here is still courtesy of the three primaries plus black!

In conclusion, if you can achieve what a commercial printer can achieve with 4 pigments, adding more should be governed by convenience not a theoretical fear that you are missing colours or saturation.

Note: The difference between ink, oil paint and watercolour paint is the support (binder) used: for ink a quick drying oil, for oil paint linseed oil and for watercolour gum Arabic. The pigments are the same.

The recommended palette

see Appendix A4 and B2, —starts with the W&N CMY trio from which a wide range of reds through orange to yellow and greens from blue to yellow are easily mixed with just two paints. Arriving reliably at colours which need all three primaries, black, browns and dark yellows, is more difficult and time consuming so, not to put off those with little or no experience with primary colour mixing, add: *'Yellow ochre – permanent, inexpensive and valuable for skies, skin, sand, and a million other applications commonly seen in nature, and Burnt Sienna for almost the same reasons as well as its magical transparency, use in adding warmth in shading and as the basis for skin'* These then are the five principle colours from which millions of others can be quickly and reliably derived. Reluctantly we include Windsor Green. This is not a natural colour and not recommended as part of the mixing palette but because of its high staining ability and high saturation it often appears in manufactured products – umbrellas,

Figure 68. Ann Monk 'Pineapple and Plums' 21" x 17" Mixed Media

Figure 69. St Emilion normal and fully saturated

tents, clothes – it has to be included. This, with Neutral tint for watercolour and charcoal grey for oil, make up the recommended palette of seven paints.

Later having learned the power and ability of the true primaries Ochre, and Burnt Sienna may be dropped. We advise that no others are acquired unless in a specific case the four fail to provide a solution, but that any additions are not included in the everyday mixing process.

Learning what the primaries can do, as soon as possible, is the quickest and surest route to achieving the colours and tones you need and the essential understanding of what paint is capable of achieving, plus it avoids biasing the end result from the adoption of an arbitrary non-primary pigment.

If we are in danger of labouring the point it is because we depart on this issue from a declining but still substantial number of educators and the majority of existing artists.

THE CORRECT PRIMARY PIGMENTS
see Appendix C

SHADING AND TINTING

Watercolour exploits both transparent colours and thinning with water to obviate the need for white paint. The same effect is produced in commercial printing by less dots of colour per given area of white paper. With oils, tinting is achieved by the

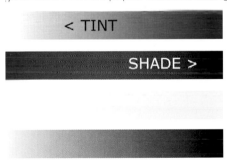

Figure 70. 'Shading Yellow with Black does not work'

The solution is to interface the two with a darker warmer Yellow, in this case Yellow Ochre

use of white paint. Tinting is intuitive and easy, there are no issues with tinting for beginners or experienced painters. There are significant issues where shading is concerned.

It is often a surprise for those new to painting to discover that Black is rarely used in either oil or watercolour painting. Black by itself tends to create ugly 'black holes'

in a painting, and when used to shade the colours, quickly makes them 'muddy'. Substitutes, other than mixing the three primaries, include Paynes Grey (too blue), Raw Umber (not quite dark enough and rather yellow), Davies Grey (too light) and Neutral Tint (in watercolour only, a formulation from W&N which hits the spot without the time needed to arrive at true neutral from the three primaries).

Beware, the use of all of these substitutes carry with them the same problems as black but to a lesser extent. *Using any of them to shade yellow, does not work*, *see Figure 70*, even if the yellow is at full strength. Shading any other colour which is not at full strength can have a similar unnatural result.

The black 'problem', or 'shading problem', is a painter's mixing and application problem. It does not occur with commercial printing. With practise of emulating the print mixing process it is possible to use black without issue – but in reality, life is too short.

The solution to the yellow problem is to mix a darker yellow but make it on the warm side, with a little more magenta or burnt sienna or use yellow ochre.

Mud is easy to achieve – mixing too many colours or any two complements will result in mud. First strengthen the colour and if still not dark enough add small amounts of neutral tint, checking that the result is not cold.

COLOUR MATCHING

Despite years of experience some colours can be very elusive. When mixing on the palette, as with achieving an exact tone in a monochrome picture, it is much easier to match a mixed colour with the reference side-by-side. This can be achieved in oil by holding the brush in line with the reference, be it from life or a photograph and in both oil and watercolour, by painting a small area on the edge of a piece of paper which can be held in line with the reference.

During the learning and practise period, try to resist modifying a reference colour. It is easy to dismiss a 'not quite right' colour or tone with 'I meant it to be that way' but to do so will not advance your colour mixing skills.

This is another one of those skills where the ability to see what is wrong is crucial and aid will help as will practise.

Tip: If you need more of a given colour do not exhaust what is on the palette, before you use it all mix next to it the additional paint. This provides an accurate side by side match.

COLOUR CO-ORDINATION

At school we were not sure what colours went with what. It takes half a lifetime for many of us to become confident not to refer to anyone else when choosing colours. We learn about colour, shape, design and style from an involuntary but constant process of selecting 'likes and dislikes'; confirming or otherwise on a day by day basis – I like that car shape, that wall colour, those shoes, that dress, etc. We can also accelerate the process where colour is concerned by reference to the designers 'colour schemes', *see Appendix C2*, collections of colours which achieve various levels of harmony or discord.

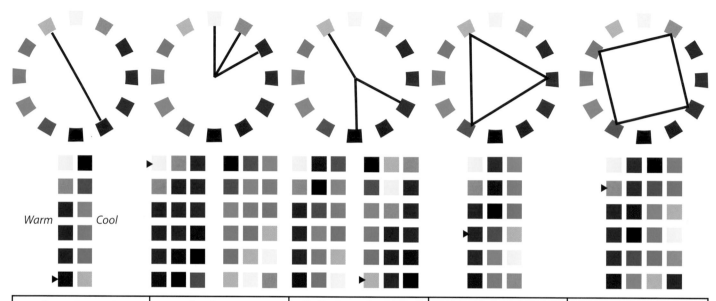

Warm   Cool

Complements	Analogous	Split Complements	Triad	Quad
Complementary colours are vibrant – handle with care can be discordant	Same strong visual contrast as complementary colours, but has less tension	Vibrant – use a triadic with one colour dominant and others as accent	Serene and comfortable – often found in nature, are harmonious and pleasing to the eye	Vibrant – best with one colour dominant

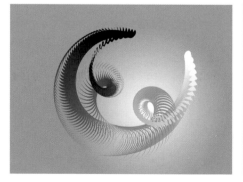

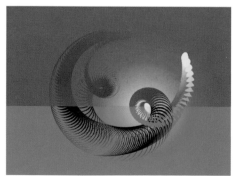

In these examples of Computer art we see the same subject with a selection of cool and warm colour treatments

Style and Stylisation

Reference photo for 'The Gondola Park'

CHAPTER IV STYLE AND STYLISATION

In this paragraph we stick our head above the parapet and make no apology for being a mite controversial.

Stylisation by technique can be achieved by over or under use of any or all of the following:

Contrast, detail, content, depth, colour, composition, perspective, atmosphere, proportion, tone, precision, medium—more or less paint, surface texture, mixed media, various effects.

Art over the centuries has had many wildly different stylisations and movements from Ancient Egyptian, Indian, Pre-Raphaelite, Renaissance, Impressionist, Surrealism, Art Nouveau, Art Deco, Religious and Nationalist art of various periods, to today's Contemporary Art, plus the styles of very many individual artists.

TUTORING

My tutoring over many years has been based on methods which have as little stylisation as possible, in the strong belief that such as there is should come naturally from the individual.

As the method of applying the paint has an impact on the end result and there are as many different methods as there are artists. The approach taken has been chosen to meet the following objectives:

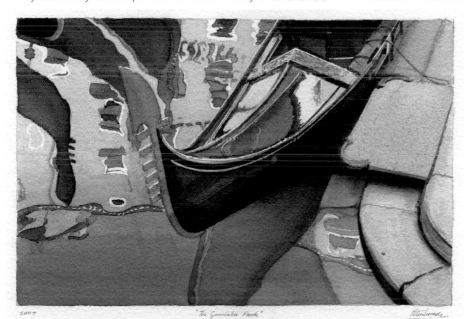

'The Gondola Park' at St Marks Square Watercolour 7" x 11" Using only the three primaries and deliberately not stylised

Tools and methods which maximise students' ability to exploit a medium with the least effort and time and which beginners can easily come to terms with

The need to stay clean – so that painting can be done in the living room

When starting to oil paint, my own studio was a distant dream. When able to live the dream, the living room was still preferred for its more sociable atmosphere.

My decision, early on, not to stylise by use of materials or their application

Everyone's work is sufficiently different without having to employ what I considered artificial or extreme techniques and no tutor should impose their style on students or produce clones of themselves. *'With practise the craft will come almost of itself, in spite of you and all the more easily if you think of something besides technique'* – Paul Gauguin. This was also influenced to some extent as a result of observation. Try as I may, none of the paintings employing exaggerated use of colour, materials or surface did anything for me. It seemed to me that those attempts to be different actually achieve the opposite, by placing them into 'Yardley like' or 'Monet like', etc. groups along with countless others.

Stylisation happens without a conscious decision to go in one direction or another. What happens when you paint is magic and it's all your own magic, or should be.

Much of contemporary art is stylised to death. In its quest to be different it has sacrificed any semblance of artistic merit. Like pornography, if there is a market there will always be suppliers. In music as in art, *'The most perfect technique is that which is not noticed at all'* – Pablo Casals.

THE CAMERA'S PLACE IN ART

The camera had as profound an impact on artists as the electric light on candle makers. Pre camera the majority of artists' incomes came from portraits, black and white photography rapidly took a large proportion of this market and the advent of colour photography took most of the remainder.

In a failed attempt at self preservation the art world mustered many arguments against photography and the feud still exists today with each alienated from and prejudiced against the other.

As a painter and photographer the arguments seem facile, but they continue to be voiced with remarkable passion and apparent conviction. In summary, artists do not consider photography an Art, *'If the man who paints only the tree, or flower, or other surface he sees before him were an artist, the king of artists would be the photographer. It is for the artist to do something beyond this'* – James Abbot McNeill Whistler, or for the broad minded few, a tool to provide a better reference than a sketch book. This is a clumsy put-down, routed in the controversial use, some 300 years before photography, of the camera obscura, which continues to be condemned by some of the less enlightened in the art world.

As a response, photographers have emphasised the camera's unique ability to capture a scene 'in a moment'. They rapidly coined the defensive phrase 'The Camera Never Lies' which, apart from never being true, undermines its claim to be an art by asserting that the skill is 'only' about the moment and that editing is not 'real' photography.

Clearly pressing a shutter is not an art. The real art in photography as in painting is in the subject choice, its composition and in the many enhancements made in content, colour and tone between the reference and the finished picture – limited only by the imagination – the same skills for photography as painting.

It is the elusive ability to see what is wrong and how to improve it that separates the artist from the copyist and the photographer from the snapper.

If the prejudices can be submerged it can be seen that the true artist and photographer share many of the same essential skills.

Before photography the sketch book was the only way a reference could be carried back to the studio. Its continued use is promoted today, as I see it, for two reasons, to encourage drawing (very laudable) and to re-enforce art's prejudice against the camera. If the reference is the priority the camera is clearly better than the sketch book, the all important speed and ability to freeze a moving subject, plus capture colour, are far superior. When used with photo-editing, pilot compositions, tonal 'sketches', black and white versions, can be completed in minutes which would otherwise take the artist hours.

Just as the brain has difficulty remembering the structure and proportions of even the most common objects, it also has difficulty visualising the consequences of changes to a composition unless a trial picture has been completed. In many cases several pilot pictures are needed before the final is arrived at. Without photo-editing this is a long, often tedious and frustrating process, so much so that it is bypassed by many at great expense to us all.

Life is by far the best reference if not the most convenient. A photo taken by the artist with a view to painting, in this day and age, is a no brainer. Those who harbour concerns really need not.

Style Influenced by Photography

In an effort to distance themselves from photography, artists, with precious few exceptions, and 'the market' have moved away from reality, in extreme cases, as far as it is possible to get. Before the camera, an artist's sketch had no value; other than to the artist. Today the majority of art for sale is closer to a sketch than to a finished painting, and most of the art being pushed by advocates of 'contemporary art' bears no relation to art as defined by history.

We do not object to enterprising individuals selling a pile of bricks to some gullible soul at far beyond their value as a pile of bricks. We do object to calling it art and to the gullible soul spending public money to purchase it.

Style today is being determined by art hijackers whose goal, as well as notoriety, is the elevation of nonentities and the creation of a market for their non art.

'Morning Light' 1971 Oil on Canvas 18" x 22" Yesteryears equivalent of the passenger jet's vapour trail high in a clear blue sky

'Winston' – 15 minute oil sketch 1965 – from a newspaper photo on the occasion of his last birthday. The photo captured the man, a picture I was compelled to paint within minutes of the newspaper delivery.

Change for Change Sake?

If a change does not improve a picture, there is no point in making it. A thought which occurs to me on many occasions when I see a wrong colour or tone or modification of nature which detracts form rather then enhances it. Yet the market for paintings which are 'photographic' is very small.

My conclusion, especially with watercolour, is the materials and the natural way in which individuals apply them, impose themselves on the end result without having to take specific steps to make further changes. In *Figure 2*, the artist's style and skill, despite his choice of watercolour, is still 'photographic'. But this is the exception, most watercolours are unmistakably watercolour and derive their popularity from being so.

In the end it should be the choice of the individual, hopefully not influenced by others. This then is where I prefer my influence to reside.

'It is no use doing what you like; you have got to like what you do' – Sir Winston Churchill.

'Armed with a paint-box, one cannot be bored, one cannot be left at a loose end, one cannot 'have several days on one's hands' – Sir Winston Churchill.

Pre Raphaelite Movement

Millais, Hunt and Rosetti, the founder members of the movement in 1848, had developed highly skilled, detailed and realistic styles. *Reproduction by Permission of the Web Gallery of Art (www.wga. hu)* They abhorred the then trend, personified, in their opinion, by Reynolds at the Royal Academy, towards an evermore formulaic 'posed' style which had started with Raphael and the Renaissance. Although their arguments gained much sympathy and ink, their timing, just prior to the explosion in photography, was unfortunate.

Movements come and go and develop extremes at the edges which mostly die, thanks to the good sense of the majority of art lovers. Today's movement, where objects of art have become a currency, will be more difficult to kill.

What is Art?

Because a self professed 'Artist', or his promoter, say it is art, doesn't make it art.

It is claimed in Clive Bell's classic essay *Art,* that art should 'stir our aesthetic emotions'. This seems to me as good a definition as any and one which holds for painting, sculpture, photography as well as ceramics, weaving, print making and a host of other artistic pursuits.

For me 'please our aesthetic emotions' would be even more appropriate. When I see work which sets out to be empty of content or ugly, discordant, obscene, deformed, disturbing, shocking, my emotions are revulsion and sadness.

While 'extremists' are in charge of art, as they are currently in so many other spheres, there will be no change and though we may sympathise with the following, they are, sad to say, probably whistling in the wind:

'I seated ugliness on my knee, and almost immediately grew tired of it' – Salvador Dali.

'A painter was asked why, since he made such beautiful figures, which were but dead things, his children were so ugly; to which the painter replied that he made his pictures by day, and his children by night' – Leonardo da Vinci.

'People are becoming increasingly bored with being shocked; in fact most of us are now shock-proof' – Jeane Duffey.

'Shock is not an enduring emotion' – Cassandra James.

'Even if unmade beds and collages of entrails are classified as art by certain circles these days, in retrospect it will be skill, imagination and originality beyond the banal and shocking that survive' – Faith Puleston.

'It's amazing what ordinary people can do if they set out without preconceived notions' Charles Franklin Kettering.

'Imagination is a very precise thing, you know – it is not fantasy; the man who invented the wheel while he was observing another man walking – that is imagination!' – Jacques Lipchitz.

'Imagination grows by exercise, and contrary to common belief, is more powerful in the mature than in the young' – W. Somerset Maugham.

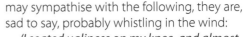

Millais

Rosetti

Hunt

First Steps

'Start as you mean to continue...'

CHAPTER V FIRST STEPS

Start as you mean to continue – that is every painting should be complete and framable. If you start with exercises you are learning to do exercises not paintings with one exception; a palette reference exercise is, like the driving instructor showing where the controls are, an invaluable first step, *see Appendix W4 and O2.*

Composition and the Viewing Frame

We are all encouraged to paint out of doors, and for good reason. It is a very rewarding if sometimes frustrating experience. *'With the changing light, movement and weather, the artist learns to paint quickly with a sense of spontaneity, making the act of painting an adventure'* – Randall Sexton.

What strikes you on your first outing, is how vast is the view. Enter the humble viewing frame; a hole, the same aspect ratio as the painting area, cut into a card. 3 Postcard size cards are ideal with cut outs of 5 x 7 inches, 6 x 9" and 7 x 11". The range of viewing angle from touching the nose – wide, to arms length – narrow, is usually sufficient. In the studio smaller frames are more appropriate, the same numbers but this time in centimetres. A viewing frame is invaluable for all subjects from life.

Framing

—is included in First Steps because getting the size correct before you draw or paint is essential to a planned composition.

To exhibit or sell, the frame will be different from your personal choice for your home. Presentation as it is called changes over time and is influenced to an extent by the exhibition or

Figure 82a. 'Normal' watercolour frame – mount no darker than this

gallery. It is wise to conform to their norm.

Watercolour Framing

The current 'norm' for watercolours is behind glass, with a wide, neutral mount – which should be the same width all round – and a thin light plain wooden frame. The objective is not to detract from the painting. No paint, gold, coloured mounts, double mounts or lines, *see Figure 82*.

Because composition makes or breaks any picture, watercolourists are strongly advised to work out the size of the painted area before they plan and draw the composition.

Base the calculations on a standard frame less the mount, less any clear space surrounding the painting and draw the box up to which you will paint.

To make life easier cut several templates, with apertures the same size as the planned painting area, which makes drawing the box much easier. Also make viewing frames to match.

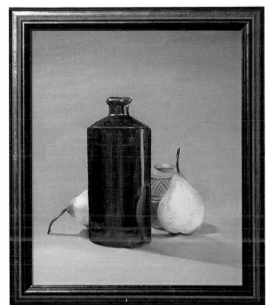

'Ink Jar with Pears' Oil on Canvas 10" x 12" Sympathetic frame enhances the painting

Figure 82b. Preferred mount style – prompts early attention to composition

An often used alternative is to use masking tape to define the painting's edges. Take care to use 'low tack' tape and be sure the tape is square and straight, not as easy as it sounds.

Oil Framing

—on the other hand, could hardly be more different, the norm being; no glass (the painting is normally varnished), if there is anything resembling a

A 'No Frame' example – Howard Birchmore's wonderful evocation of the sea

mount, most often not, it will be thin and usually black, white or gold. The frame itself, often large and colourful, is chosen by a professional framer to 'enhance the painting' – a rare talent.

Why they are so different, no one has yet provided a convincing explanation.

Oil painters need to check that standard frames are available for the canvases or canvas boards they are being offered.

No Frame for Oils

Because of the difficulty and expense of framing oils, it has become acceptable to sell without a frame. For this purpose canvases are available with no staples on the sides and with very neat corners. The painting may or may not wrap around the top bottom and sides.

Standard v Custom Cost

You will want to frame your pictures sooner than you expect – and if you do not your partner probably will. Unless you take the following advice you will be in for a somewhat rude awakening, assuming you do not like to throw money down the drain that is. Standard frames cost between £4 and £15 for the size we are interested in at an early stage of our development. The same pictures in a custom frame costs between £30 and £50.

MATERIALS—Economy v Quality

Paint

It is false economy to purchase 'student quality' paints. The key to learning to paint is remembering what a given set of paints will do in concert with each other. Any subsequent change will result in much re-learning. All of the compromises made to reduce the cost of paints reduce their quality and have a negative impact on the final work.

Watercolour Brushes

The difference between a good quality sable and a synthetic brush, is like comparing cashmere and polyester. Another area where economy is not appropriate.

As a rule of thumb, the largest size capable of managing the needed detail is the most appropriate, usually size 8 to 10.

Among the best quality and value is the Escoda: Kolinsky-Tajmyr Sable round watercolour brush series 1212 (ferrule diameter 4.3mm, Hair Length 22mm) – Size 8. The measurements are needed to compare between makers whose number sizes are not consistent.

Size 8 is good for all but medium to large areas of wash, where a size 16 round synthetic is recommended.

Testing a Watercolour Brush

The makers ship brushes with a coating of gum arabic. This preserves the shape and point but it means, until the gum arabic is washed out, you are unable to assess its quality.

Having soaked the brush and removed all trace of gum, 'throw' the access water off and a good brush will come to a single sharp point, will not look bent and no odd hairs will be apparent.

Only the brush on the left is good

Watercolour Paper

The two to one range in price doesn't necessarily reflect two to one in quality. Whilst the most expensive is probably the best the least is also good quality but different in its materials and manufacture. Bockingford is half the price of Arches but both are good. Bockingford is whiter but softer and more absorbent, Arches is 100% cotton, has a harder more resilient coating, better disposed to scratching, scraping and rework in general.

Start with the best but try several and choose whichever suits your style.

Paper thickness and price are roughly in proportion. The popular inexpensive 140lb papers are thin, need stretching and dry quickly. Personally I would pay any price to avoid these limitations. Choose a 300lb paper, or heavier, for large (much beyond 24") pictures. Avoiding the need for stretching is the main reward but extended drying time is also invaluable, *see Appendix W1 – Paper.*

Canvas and Oil Boards

Most of the art surfaces currently available are made in China, including many from the big name brands. The quality has been variable to say the least. A canvas or board with a visible knot or join is a reject, as are boards which do not stay flat. Sadly these have been common occurrences in recent years so buyer beware, regardless of the name brand.

Linen is the best but cotton, the most common, is perfectly good and long lasting. The quality of the coating is variable, the worst being capable of removal if rubbing out is too aggressive.

These materials are in a state of flux. Given that most of the costs are remarkably low, the best advice is lots of trial and error, *see Appendix O1.*

Oil Brushes

Not as important or expensive as watercolour, synthetics for the soft types are perfectly OK. The stiff ones really should be made from a quality Hog's Hair. Determining what is quality and what is not, I for one have yet to master, so the guide (not always reliable) has to be name brand and price.

Easels

An easel is not necessary for watercolour either in or out of doors. A light weight foam board or cardboard sheet two to three inches larger than the paper is ideal.

The common light, portable easels are frustratingly wobbly but unavoidable when oil painting out of doors.

In doors, beyond the two chair solution, the most solid, least wobbly, studio easel you can afford is the best choice for oil painting, if you have the space – check for headroom.

Those with a facility to attach a rest for the palette are my personal choice.

Palettes

Disposable palettes for oil and plastic 'combination' palettes for watercolour are areas appropriate for economy; the least expensive are perfectly adequate.

Oil Solvent

An additional expense with oil is the brush wash and general cleaning up agent. At roughly the same price as whisky and considering the constant washing and cleaning that is required it would be nice to think that there was a less expensive alternative. Unfortunately the other solutions are far less effective as solvents. Distilled Turpentine is the most effective, even the slightly less expensive Pure Turpentine is not as good and all of the substitutes are hopeless.

However, there is a tip to make the solvent go further. At the end of a session all of the brushes need to be thoroughly cleaned, see Brush Cleaning. The pigment that remains in the jar will settle to a firm sediment, enabling the clean solvent to be poured off into a second jar for subsequent re-use.

Note: Olive oil is good at removing oil paint from clothes – then you will need to remove the olive oil...

In the Studio – Tripod Studio Easel – solid and flexible (not too high for large canvases), with high chair – behind is a 'wobbly' field easel for oils out of doors

Tuscany with little and with improved colour depth, recalls our trip on 9/11 and several perfect days in this haven far from New York

Constable 'The Cornfield' (detail) © National Gallery, London – what a difference a sky makes – the depth is achieved with both colour and size perspective

TONE DRAWING

Doing a tone drawing prior to a painting is a quick and efficient way to check the overall composition. Certainly it is better than discovering a compositional problem after completing the painting.

DEPTH AND COLOUR PERSPECTIVE

Essentially depth is preserved by making things smaller the further away they are and by observing colour perspective.

Water

Water is a special case in that we view it mostly at very acute angles. The foreshortening of a 25 foot wave half a mile away is about as high as a pencil lead and half way to the horizon it is hair thick. Also because of the angle and the uneven surface, objects like clouds do not get reflected in water. If the angle is changed, such as viewing from an aeroplane, then like a mirror we do see the clouds.

A brush can't hope to define the fine detail of ripples half a mile away. The solution is a smooth graduated wash kept as horizontal as possible.

For the same reason, any highlights or sparkles in the water must get smaller the further away they are – easy with oil, not so easy with watercolour. The impression is created by employing several effects, *see Appendix W1.*

Failure to implement this kills the sense of depth that every two dimensional picture needs.

Clouds

Most pictures with clouds are enhanced by making them larger and brighter in the foreground going to smaller and less bright with distance. Even if the reference did not at the time have clouds in the distance.

Trees

—are another case for treatment. If the distance is beyond the brushes capability to define the branch structure, never settle for thicker branches,

'The Magnac Fuel Store' 1992 Watercolour 3 1/2" x 2 1/4" One of a series of miniatures of the Author's French home – actual size

just blur the shape of the tree.

Depth achieved by colour perspective has also to be reckoned with. Compare the darks in the distance with the darks in the foreground. The greater the difference the greater is the sense of atmosphere and depth. Colours are lighter and less saturated in the distance.

TONE

—is another aspect of drawing and painting where some people seem to be able to get it right without much trouble or thought and others struggle, even to see what is wrong.

Tone is simply the amount of light and shade or contrast in a picture – ignore colour, what is left is tone. Getting tones correct, like the other skills, has to be learned and practised. Helping to see what is wrong is part of that process, see Side-by-side below.

Side-by-side comparison

Our ability to match a tone, like matching a colour, is significantly improved with side-by-side comparison. Hold a paper with the approximate tone painted at the edge, against the life or photo reference.

Note: Looking at the drawing or painting up-side-down helps to see what may be wrong with both tone and colour. The brain tends to disconnect from the subject and can concentrate more on colour and tonal values.

EXERCISE—THE PALETTE REFERENCE

Exercises in general, teach how to do exercises rather than complete paintings but there are a couple which have value, especially at the start of the painting process. First is the palette reference, *see Appendix W4 and O2.*

When new to a set of paints or when a paint is added to a palette, it is very helpful to produce a reference to the colours: How they look without modification and when tinted to white and shaded to black. Plus an initial experience of mixing the secondary colours and black from the three primaries. To mix exact colours takes a great deal of practise so do not expect too much of your first efforts. If you are a 'natural' you may arrive at what you want quite early on, including the difficult black. Most of us will find blacks and browns time consuming and frustrating, hence the addition of brown (Burnt Sienna) and black (Neutral Tint for watercolour and Charcoal Grey or Raw Umber for oil) to the recommended palette.

The second exercise is to master the watercolour wash, see Graduated Wash – *page 43.*

'Composition, the aim of which is expression, alters itself according to the surface to be covered. If I take a sheet of paper of given dimensions, I will jot down a drawing which will have a necessary relation to its format' – Henri Matisse.

'The Magnac Pottery' 1992 Watercolour 3 1/2" x 2 1/4" A challenge in colour and tone captures the sun's warmth reflected from the 1750 barn

Watercolour Technique

*'challenging,
unforgiving and
very rewarding'*

CHAPTER VI WATERCOLOUR TECHNIQUE

Before we move on it is as well to point out that the pen has its limitations when seeking to describe how to accomplish hand-eye co-ordination processes. A book may be part of the learning but by itself is not sufficient. No one learned to drive a car (or paint) from a book alone. Making real headway requires demonstrating, tutoring and doing – lots and lots of doing.

Space does not allow coverage of all the many watercolour techniques. We cover the most used and the most valuable, *see also Appendix W4* – Watercolour Effects.

GETTING STARTED

The two principal types of watercolour paints are, Tubes and Pans, tubes are the

'Coffee Time' 2006 Watercolour 7" x 11" This literal translation is an indication of watercolour's ability with strength of tone and colour

more popular, economy, life and availability are all generally better with tubes, the key however is to use tubes in the same way that pans are used. Into the colour wells of a combination palette, *see Appendix W 3*, squeeze 1/2" from each tube into six wells. The lightest paint, yellow, bottom left to the darkest, Neutral Tint, top right. Keeping empty wells next to the Yellows and Red helps keep the paints clean.

This makes six colours from left to right – Yellow (Winsor Yellow), Yellow Ochre, Red [Magenta] (Permanent Rose). *Blue [Cyan] (Winsor Blue-Green shade), Brown (Burnt Sienna) and Black [dark Grey] (Neutral Tint).

*Note: There should be a space left in case you ever need Green (Winsor Green-Yellow shade) between the red and blue.

Watercolour technique is a process of building up transparent (staining) layers. Never apply thick paint as in most other paint mediums. Thick paint will 'smear' when subsequent layers are applied.

The pigment sits on the surface and the water soaks into the paper. It is easy to make things dark but difficult, after they have dried, to make them lighter; for this reason, watercolours progress from light to dark, rarely if ever the other way.

Shading is applied after the base colour has dried. Most tinting on the other hand is accomplished while the paint is still wet.

Graduated tinting is achieved by several techniques:

1. Make what has just been applied, go further – apply the paint, dry the brush (draw it toward you across a quadrupled layer of kitchen roll) and drag the wet paint, achieving a thinner, lighter result until the paint is too dry to go any further.

2. If there is a hard line between the paint and the white paper, and there usually is, quickly clean and dry the brush and 'lift off' the edge. Both processes must be done while the paint is still wet.

3. An alternative to 2 above is to clean and almost dry the brush then apply the damp brush to the white paper just to one side of the edge and allow the paint at the edge to seep onto the now damp paper.

Surprises

If too wet, various drying surprises* will result and a smooth transition will be difficult or impossible to achieve.

*Hard edge – the pigment forms a line between the wet and dry areas of the paper.

*Granulation – the pigment settles into the grain of the paper.

*Wet-in-wet flooding – a wet area, or brush, will flood into a less wet area.

Your first experience of all of this is similar to the first few hours of car driving – the whole thing seems impossible – but persevere, the control of how much water and pigment is the essence of watercolour painting and like driving, the penny doesn't drop in five minutes.

Graduated Wash

The process of achieving a smooth graduation from white paper to a full strength colour is not easy and gets more difficult as the area increases. A typical sky, dark blue above fading to nothing at the horizon has to be complete in seconds if the clouds, which are dabbed out, are to be white rather than blue. To an extent discontinuities can be hidden under the clouds. The sea is less forgiving, the wash has to be smooth if the needed depth is to be preserved. This graduated wash is one of watercolour's most demanding techniques, only exceeded by having to avoid a complicated foreground subject along the way.

Practise, as always, makes perfect, several practise pads full of washes are needed before this particular penny drops and although there may be doubters long into the learning process – it can be done, *see also Appendix W2, Water.*

Speed is vital – A second or two

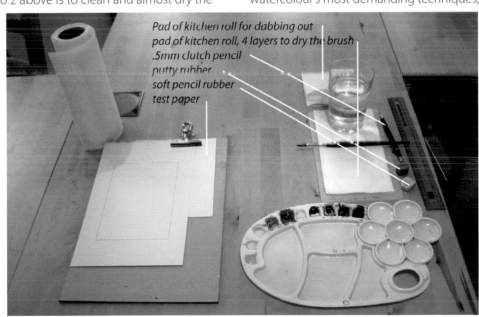

Pad of kitchen roll for dabbing out
pad of kitchen roll, 4 layers to dry the brush
.5mm clutch pencil
putty rubber
soft pencil rubber
test paper

Watercolour set up – because the painting is forever being rotated, a heavy drawing board is not helpful. Cardboard or foamboard is better and less expensive. Some prefer, with 300lb+ papers, to use only the paper

can make the difference between a smooth transition and an objectionable discontinuity,

especially if you make the mistake of going back on yourself.

A valuable extension of working time can be had by the use of thicker papers and for some, by wetting the area before applying the paint, but selective wetting stimulates hard edge, and makes it more difficult to judge how wet or dry the paper is and therefore when to start painting.

Wetting the back of the paper all over can be effective but again your judgement on when to start painting is critical.

Other techniques involve working on a pad of damp blotting paper – what is 'damp' is once more the big question. Then there is the environment, a damp cool room extends the working time relative to a hot dry one.

The Wash

Washes, even with practise, have a habit of 'going wrong'. To guard against the risk of ruining an otherwise good foreground, the general watercolour rule of proceeding from light to dark, is sometimes ignored.

There are two basic types of large area wash, *see Appendix W 1*, A smooth graduated wash, as in skies and seas, are best done with the paper near horizontal with great care not to return to the wash with too wet a brush. Most problems, drying surprises, hard edge and flooding, with this type of wash are because things are too wet.

At the top of the wash area, lay down a broad band of dark and wet paint but immediately proceed to drag it down and make it go as far as possible getting thinner and dryer as it

descends. Now the brush is exhausted and needs to be refilled, this time with a weaker mixture of pigment and with much of the wetness removed by dabbing the brush onto the pad of kitchen roll. Make the next stroke just below where you left off, to avoid flooding upwards, and when this stroke is done, merge the two bands and continue to make the bottom of the second band go further. This is now repeated with less and less pigment to the bottom of the wash area. All this needs to be done in 5 to 10 seconds.

Note: To avoid making a minor discontinuity worse, never go back on yourself during a wash, the solution is to get it right first time or make a correction when the wash is dry.

Practise, practise, practise.

Dabbing

When you 'dab out' the clouds from several graduated sky washes, you will soon recognise what a difference a few seconds makes. Dabbing out, or lifting off, as the words imply, involves forming a pad of kitchen roll and applying it to the wet wash to form the clouds, a very effective and satisfying technique. The same process can be used to obtain light reflections in a sea or river scene.

'Scales' 2006 Watercolour 8" x 11" The depth of colour here is achieved by layering

Wet Vertical Wash

Hold the paper near vertical and this time with a strong very wet mixture (mix two or three times more than you think you will need because to run out mid wash is to ruin it), stroke, starting at the top, in smooth horizontal lines, developing as you go a wave, horizontal very wet band at the bottom of the wash – if not enough it will not work, if too much it could run. Top up the wave from the mix and continue descending, working either side of the foreground subject, staying level

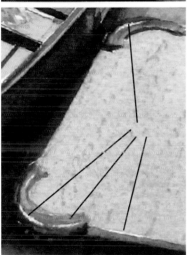

Figure 95. Before and after Scratching

and horizontal. Close to the bottom, make the wave go further so that it is exhausted just at the bottom of the wash area.

This type of wash cannot be graduated, but a graduated wash can be applied on top after it is dry.

Scratching

—is the use of a craft knife or better a scalpel to remove selected areas of pigment, to restore what should have been white paper. Note: The paper must be very dry. The recommended method is to use many light scratches so as not to dig into the paper, finish the process with an eraser. The result will not be as clean an edge as is possible by leaving white paper but it is a common finishing process for many watercolours, *see Figure 95*.

Scraping

—is the use of the flat of the scalpel blade to remove pigment from the tops of the paper's textured surface. This is effective in producing multiple highlights in say foamy water or the sun's reflection on water or a foreground where the whites can be subsequently painted as pebbles or other textured surfaces. With patience quite large areas can be successfully removed, *see Figure 96*.

Skimming

—is the inverse of scraping. The side of a brush is drawn over the surface of the paper so that just the top of the paper's texture is painted. The brush has to be nearly dry to achieve the best result. When used to give the impression of foamy or rippled water it can be very effective.

Note: Both scraping and skimming are only effective over a narrow band of the pictures depth. If applied in the distance and in the foreground, because the texture is the same, the depth, which should be achieved by making everything smaller in the distance, is lost.

Masking Fluid

—can be used to preserve white paper

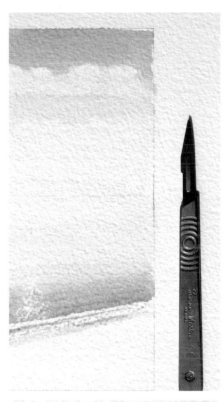

Figure 96. Foamy water and reflections achieved by Skimming, reflections and white tops of the clouds by Scraping. Water and sky started with graduated washes.

highlights if you are not convinced that the white paper can be 'left' which is the preferred solution, for example the poppy heads in a poppy field.

Because the fluid is a brush killer the use of sticks, tooth picks, etc. are often advised, making it difficult to get the masking exactly where it is needed. Better would be to buy a job lot of very small brushes and accept that they will be disposable.

The Egg Shell Effect

If when an egg is painted it has 'contour lines' the egg effect will be lost. It's easy to set-up a still life with eggs and sundry other items and is very good early practise in putting paint on then lifting it off, letting it dry, then repeating the process, building up colour, tone and modelling. This technique applies to a vast array of subjects in watercolour, including; faces, figures, petals; anything which must be smooth and rounded.

To 'lift off' the brush needs to be dryer than the area you are working on. If it is wetter the contents of the brush will 'flood' into the area. This is called wet-in-wet.

Wet-in-Wet

Some interesting results come from this technique, yet another which needs a lot of

'Champagne' 7 1/2" x 4 1/2" close to life size, a 'loose' (for me) example of watercolour

practise. It is often used in backgrounds and in cloud effects, wet-in-wet is difficult to control and repeatability is not a strength, happy and unhappy accidents abound. Flooding, which occurs when the brush is wetter than the surface, is usually destructive, damp in damp is probably a better way to describe what is needed.

Stippling

—is using the point of the brush to produce leaves, one point to produce one leaf or make the brush form multiple points by bouncing it on a hard surface – not too wet – results in many leaves painted at the same time; an old brush with a worn point is ideal. The same technique can be used for bushes and various textured surfaces.

Sponge

A natural sponge can be used to dab out and to apply paint. A sponge with the widest variation of texture is best for creating a range of size and depth.

Try and practise them all and come to your own conclusions

which suit you best. Even invent your own as most watercolour painters do. Finding and using effects is one of watercolour's most creative and challenging features.

Cotton Wool Bud

Dry watercolour can be removed selectively by using a damp cotton wool bud. Damp not wet, if unwelcome surprises are to be avoided. The result is soft highlights and / or minor corrections. *See Appendix A4* for a list of effects.

When to Relax

Not everything in watercolour has to be done in a hurry. There is a tendency to rush on at breakneck speed but planning ahead, mixing and most execution, need time and should be done at your leisure.

'Translucence is an effect unique to the medium of watercolour and the lure that beckons me into the studio for yet another creative adventure' – Michele Cooper.

'Everything about watercolour appeals to me, but perhaps above all, the peculiarities of the medium tend to challenge my efforts to control it... it's more like a performance or a dance' – John Hulsey.

'Watercolour is like golf, every stroke counts...' – Katie Wood McCloy.

'It is remarkable how very individual technique becomes in watercolour. Every man of personality finally arrives at a method peculiarly his own, as unique as his own fingerprint' – Walter J. Phillips.

'In watercolour, if you are not in trouble, then you're in trouble' – Selma Blackburn.

'Batailley 1961' Watercolour 8" x 6" In some paintings liberties can be taken with colour but in this case the wine colour must be spot on – note: In this close-up, which adds intimacy, some vertical perspective has been used

This study is good practise to perfect smooth graduations, important for so many watercolour subjects and so often used in the studio, we now call it the egg shell technique

Oil Technique

'wet-in-wet fast and flexible'

CHAPTER VII OIL TECHNIQUE

In meeting our objective of 'the colour we want where we want it', wet-in-wet – the method we describe here – is the quickest process. The painting is completed in one session without waiting for anything to dry. This technique is what makes oil painting so different from the other paint mediums, blending and changes can be made over an extended period. It is also the process which causes existing watercolour painters the most anguish.

Wet-in-wet oil painting, is about as effective a colour medium to achieve the objective, as there is. From real via impressionist to abstract, from wall sized to miniatures, it combines strength of colour with the most powerful ability to blend on the canvas and

Figure 101. Application by area—cover the territory with the colours and tones required then blend and add detail

make changes over several hours. In short it is the colour medium most capable of achieving what you want where you want it. Wet-in-wet is also less prone to cracking than the alternative layering methods.

Its disadvantages, the difficulty of painting fine light structures onto a wet background, the potential for mess and where transport is unavoidable plus the time taken to dry, can be mitigated by method and planning.

'Oil paint is sensuous and I find it highly seductive. Like life' – Ann Dettmer.

Staying 'Plague' free

Oil paintings greatest single drawback is the ease by which the painter can get covered in oil paint. When a painter finds paint where it shouldn't be it is probable that it will also be in many other places, on your hand, brush handle, clothes, etc. We call this the 'Plague'. It is very easy to get the plague, it must be taken seriously and its avoidance and treatment need to be learned, practised and mastered. We do not recommend the use of rags at any stage, they are too absorbent and actually help to transmit the plague.

Brush Cleaning

—is an unavoidable pain if you wish to use oils to the maximum of their capability.

Distilled turpentine is the only solvent recommended, despite its price at about the same as whisky.

To clean a brush between colours, squeeze most of the paint onto a square of paper, newspaper is too absorbent, magazines are not absorbent enough, phone books are ideal, four squares per page is a good size. Discard the paper after one or two squeeze and pull actions. Now touch the brush on the surface of some distilled turpentine, the brush soaks up the turpentine, then, on a folded paper square, draw the brush towards you, with a rocking / rotating movement, liberating the remaining paint. This stage needs to be repeated until the brush is clean. Finally squeeze out all of the thinners.

Tedious? Yes but more effective and cleaner than any of the other methods.

Transporting Wet Oils

Planning to transport one or several wet oils, involves the manufacture or purchase of a carrier capable of keeping the paintings separated and secure throughout a car or aeroplane journey. This is not easy – the carrier needs to be adjustable to cope with your chosen size of picture and with boards as well as stretchers. Variable sizes

make the proposition all but impossible.

This issue is at its most significant when returning from an oil painting holiday with say 6 to 12 wet pictures.

Acrylic devotees will claim quick drying as a major advantage over oil as far as transport is concerned and they would be right, but this does not compensate for losing the ability to make changes for hours which quick drying prohibits. Yes you can now buy acrylics which dry slowly – just like oils?

Assume the Position

Painting with oil has for the past several hundred years, been completed with the canvas or board vertical or near vertical. This helps separate the wet canvas from the painter and assists in avoiding the plague. For most of us it means learning a different way of applying the paint. Writing, drawing and most other painting is done with the surface close to or actually horizontal, with part of the hand resting for support on the

Figure 101b. 'Black and Terracotta' Oil on Canvas 10" x 12"
A painting from life with careful thought given to colour and composition

paper, which is in turn on a board. For the best control we work close to the surface with very little distance between the end of the fingers and the tip of the brush or pencil. Because in oil we can't touch a wet canvas we have to find other means of control and support. Oil is painted 'at a distance', which is why oil brushes have long handles.

Standing

A common approach has been to stand in front of an easel, with the left hand holding a palette, several brushes and / or maybe a maulstick, and the right hand doing the painting. In this mode the right hand and arm are unsupported and tend to 'wander', i.e. not much support or control. Some improvement can be gained by pressing the right elbow into the body or touching the palette onto the right wrist. Even more by using a maulstick or a second paint brush as a rest.

Variations include; the palette and brushes on a side table or the palette on an attachment to the easel, now the left hand can support the painting hand and both elbows can rest on the trunk. In all cases the brush is held well down the long brush handle with the tip of the brush between 4 and 8 inches from the finger tips, add to this the ability to paint at arms length and the painter can be as much as 3 feet from the canvas or as little as 6 inches, with the added advantage of the ability to immediately walk backward and see as seen by the audience. Just as we 'stand back' to appreciate many paintings so the artist has also to stand back to create them.

Sitting

Standing for hours at a time is not for everyone. This can be the same as all of the above but somewhat less mobile and at the sitting height of a standard or high chair / stool.

Chair Replaces Easel

A variation to sitting is to abandon the easel and side table and opt for two high backed chairs, one to sit on with the other performing both the easel and side table functions, see the photos. This setup has many advantages and is the one I have used for the past 40+ years. The support available from

Relaxed and controlled painting at an Oil class

First Oil for this student

sitting with elbows on knees and the left hand supporting the right affords excellent control and is comfortable over many hours. Because all you need is contained in front of you on a stable chair the risk of plague is reduced. The need to purchase a wobbly or expensive large easel is avoided and, after a little practise, oil painting can be done in the living room using minimal space.

Two Chairs Set Up

Note: Many of the recommendations here are to avoid the plague and keep you and the painting area clean.

The oil boards are mounted onto stiff card or foam board using pea size BlueTack at each corner. This allows vertical adjustment of the painting, preventing the sleeve or wrist from touching the palette. The larger board also prevents the chair from being painted.

Also to keep the chair clean and provide a flat surface, the seat has first a piece of cardboard, large enough to keep the palette (A4 size), with dipper attached for brush wash, a stack of one time use papers (yellow pages cut into 4), a palette knife – to move the paint around the palette, pencil, putty rubber and a brush or maximum two brushes. Too many brushes help generate the plague.

Brushes and the palette knife should be cleaned before they are put down, *see Page 49* Brush Cleaning.

A large cardboard box on your left should be available for the used papers – don't screw them up, just drop them.

For those shorter than average height a solution is required to keep the distance from the floor to your knee high enough for the wrist not to get too close to the paint. Prop the heal against the chair, or use a foot rest.

If (or when) you get paint on your hands, don't use the one time papers, they are not absorbent enough, remove the paint with a small amount of brush wash on a folded square of kitchen roll.

Table Easel

If you suffer from a bad back or simply can't get on with the methods described above, as a last resort – because it is farthest from traditional oil painting – try using a table easel. You will be sitting upright with elbows on the table, so control is good, the palette between you and the easel and as far from the canvas as is comfortable.

Canvas or board?

Canvas boards are less expensive, easier to frame and offer a stable, non flexible, surface. Having said that, if you want to sell your work, the gallery or buyer will expect it to be on a stretcher, i.e. its value is at its best on a 'proper' canvas.

Do's and Don'ts

Do work with the canvas vertical or close to vertical, for this you will need an easel or the two chair method previously described. Treat the canvas and the end of the brush as though they were red hot, i.e. not to be touched. This is traditional technique and there is no reason not to employ it. In turn this means not holding the brush, as with horizontal writing or sketching, too close to the sharp end. Note that oil brush handles are longer to facilitate this.

Do not dilute oil paint.

Do not overpaint or underpaint a reference line.

Do use just enough paint to cover the canvas—too little is considered poor practice, too much makes blending and wet-on-wet detail much more difficult.

Oil Technique is unlike watercolour where there seems to be a technique for everything. Apart from mastering 1. Application by area, 2. Blending on the canvas and 3. Fine detail, oil is virtually technique free. The answer most of the time is 'paint what you see'.

Application by Area

If an area on the painting has a different colour or tone, paint it as a separate area, for all but the most subtle differences. The result prior to blending should look rather like a contour map, *see Page 48 Figure 101*. At this early stage, never countenance putting one paint on top of another, this is watercolour technique not oil.

Blending on the canvas

Numerous objects that we paint are based upon a core colour, e.g. a face—skin colour. A tree—green. In most cases however there are many shades of the core colour. The technique to achieve these many colours is to mix on the palette a skin colour which represents the lightest that can be seen, and the darkest with sometimes one or two in between, then blend the many tones between these few paints on the canvas. When the 'modelling' has been completed to your satisfaction, then add the really subtle other colours which make up the face, redder cheeks, bluer around the eyes, etc. Blending each new paint into the existing core tones. The same process is applicable to trees, petals, grass, sky blues, and countless others.

Detail with oil

In wet-in-wet the use of smaller more pointed brushes does not achieve the detail we might expect. Smaller fine brushes produce shorter lines especially light on dark. The effective technique is to apply more paint where the fine line is needed and trim the access either side of the line with the darker paint. With this 'push' technique, smooth accurate edges and fine lines

Detail without the use of a small brush

can be achieved with practise. An aid to this approach is to leave blank canvas where highlights are needed. Their position is retained and subsequent application of the lighter colour is much easier (quicker).

Oil Paint Consistency

Oil painting technique is very different in comparison to the other colour mediums, especially those taught at school. If a bead of white paint is placed onto a vertical canvas next to a bead of black, there is no interaction, one does not blend into the other and neither will run or move until the painter, more like sculpturing, pushes and blends them together. This consistency, not too thin that the paints run and not thick as to become sticky, should be the same for all of the colours.

The makers work hard to achieve this and we dilute them, with either brush wash or oil, at our peril. It is the variations in the amount of brush wash (thinners) and oil between colours on a painting that causes it to crack, as each will dry (contract) at a different rate. If you wish to under paint, also called glazing, with oil, simply make the paint go further, do not make it thinner.

Occasionally when a tube is squeezed its support (linseed oil), having separated in the tube from the pigment, will run out leaving a thicker sticky paint. There are two solutions, first replace the cap and squeeze the tube so that the contents re-mixes. If this does not fully work (often the case), add, on the palette, a small amount of refined linseed oil to bring the paint back to its original consistency. This is the only time linseed oil is needed during painting.

Note: Some of the text books have a hard time recommending this, as many painters in the past, in ignorance of the cause of premature cracking, have diluted oil paints.

When layering, with drying between layers, it is often recommended to apply 'fat on thin'. This means that subsequent layers should have increasing amounts of oil in order to reduce the likelihood of cracking.

There are other methods and as many variations as there are artists. What we present here has been developed to get the first time oil painter to master the medium as quickly and efficiently as possible. Along the way we will all adopt variations which suit us best and help make our work distinctive and identifiable.

Dear Reader

This has been a distillation of much that I have learned over the years, from many students and my own efforts. I hope all readers will find value in it and the encouragement to take up painting sooner rather than later.

Sincerely

Peter Turner

APPENDIX W1 – Watercolour

Care of materials
- Brushes – avoid fracturing even a single hair – never hit the bottom of the water jar
- Paints – from tubes to palette – top up each colour as needed
- Each watercolour needs to be instantly available and should be softened with a drop of water at each session
- Never mix in the colour wells
- Take colour from colour wells only with a clean brush

Mixing
- Plastic 'Combination Palette' Wheatsheaf ART-316A
- Start with nearest colour. More colours = more mute – more mud
- Mix of any two complementary colours = black
- Use of black is not recommended – makes colours 'dirty' or 'muddy' and used by itself creates 'black holes' in the painting
- Damp (not wet) paper extends the 'working time' – some use damp blotting paper under damp paper – use even less liquid on the brush. Results are unpredictable
- Heavy papers extend working time

Paper
—Acid free and 'coated' (sized) both sides – coating retains paint on the surface and enhances colours.

Weight: LB g/m2 gsm	90lb 185gsm Stretch	140lb 300gsm Use block, Stretch?	300lb 638gsm No need to stretch

Paper and Picture Size

Size	FRAME IN	FRAME MM	Mount Aperture	Picture IN
	7 x 5	187 x 127	None*	4 1/2 x 2 1/4
	8 x 6	203 x 152	None*	5 x 3
	8 x 8	203 x 203	None*	5 x 5
	10 x 7	254 x 178	7 x 4	6 x 3
	10 x 8	254 x 203	6 x 4	5 x
A4	8 1/4 x 11 3/4	210 x 297	7 3/4 x 4 1/4	6 3/4 x 3 1/4
	10 x 10	254 x 254	6 x 6	5 x 5
A3	11 3/4 x 16 1/2	420 x 297	7 3/4 x 12 1/2	6 3/4 x 11 1/2
A2	16 1/2 x 23 3/8	420 x 591	11.5 x 16 3/8	10 1/2 x 15 3/8
	12 x 9	305 x 229	8 x 5	7 x 4
	12 x 10	305 x 254	8 x 6	7 x 5
	14 x 10	355 x 254	10 x 6	9 x 5
	14 x 11	355 x 280	10 x 7	9 x 6**
	16 x 12	410 x 310	12 x 8	11 x 7
	18 x 14	457 x 356	13 x 9	12 x 8
	20 x 14	510 x 360	14 x 8	13 x 7
	20 x 16	508 x 406	15 x 11	14 x 10
	24 x 18	610 x 460	17 x 11	16 x 10
Sheets	29 x 22	737 x 559	20 x 13	19 x 12

Half Sheet 22 x 14.5, Quarter sheet 14.5 x 11, 1/8 Sheet 11 x 7.25
*Paper = Frame size
**Good economic choice and aspect ratio 8 pictures 9 x 6" per sheet, 14 x 11 standard frame

Notes:
   Frame Size refers to the glass size, not the inside or outside measurement of the frame

   Sheets are available from most art shops. This is mould made standard size quite large for shopping in the high street. When ordered from jacksonsart.co.uk you may request them to be cut in halves or quarters before shipping

Coating
   (glue size)—is applied by submersing the sheet so that painting may be done on either side depending on the choice of surface texture. Each maker has a slightly different texture per side.

Picture Size
   We learn as much from a picture 5" x 7" as one double the size but the larger picture will take up to four times as long to complete. Handling detail also requires more practise than quick rough execution. The more complete pictures done in the early stages of learning the better. By this process all of the skills are practised. This doesn't need to be taken too far, every now and then, perhaps every 10th painting should be larger, so that the differences are appreciated.

Paper Cutting
   Even if you ask the supplier to cut the sheets, or you find a supply of good 300lb paper in the form of a book, you will still want to make smaller sizes and / or trim the paintings.

   Safe and efficient paper cutting calls for the use of specific tools. The cutter should be a Stanley knife, most other craft knives are too small or too flimsy. Use only a metal, aluminium or steel, rule preferably with a non-skid surface on the bottom and at least 24 inches long. This is important if your fingers or a plastic rule are not to be cut. The cutting surface can be cardboard but it will not last long and there is a danger of the blade cutting the table. Better but much more expensive is a plastic cutting board on top of an MDF drawing board, both at least 24" on the long side. Note: The costly cutting board can easily be cut through.

Mount Cutting
   Using the same boards and rule, mounts can successfully cut by hand but the only mount cutter I can recommend is the American made Logan Graphic Products Inc. Push Style mat cutter model 2000 using blade number 270. Be sure to place a waste piece of mount board under each cut. If you cut onto a plastic cutting board the blade is likely to loose its point, i.e. break off.

APPENDIX W2 – Watercolour Continued

Paper Cont. Surface – Choose from Three:

Smooth HP (Hot Pressed) Botanic work	Normal NOT (Not HP) Recommended	Rough Larger works

Makers:

Langton – Daler-Rowney – available, good selection / price – no 300 lb
Arches – French – available, 100% cotton, the best, 90 and 140 lb
– blocks, pads and sheets inc. 300 lb – wm/d
Bockingford – good when available – sheets 72, 140 and 250 lb and pads of 140 lb
Saunders Waterford – 100% cotton – e.g. 638 gsm (300 lb) Sheets each wm/d
Whatman – rag – up to 400 gsm (200 lb) sheets – d
(prices are from a typical high street artshop)
wm = watermark / d = rough edges (deckle)

Brushes – Scale

- Increase brush size with the scale of the work, e.g. painting area 5" x 7" – 8 to 10 for most work – difficulty in controlling fine detail may impose a reduced size 3 – 6. Avoid small brushes, they do not retain enough paint and encourage overworking.
- Quality (price) most expensive retain more paint and shape for longer, e.g.
- Escoda: Kolinsky-Tajmyr Sable Round Watercolour Brush Series 1212 (ferrule diameter 4.3mm, Hair Length 22mm) – Size 8 The only 'branded' brush at a reasonable price or...
Jackson's Red Sable size: 5 – 8 – 10
- W & N are much more expensive, e.g. Series 7 size 8 (equivalent to size 10 for most other makers) is 10 times the price.
- For washes we recommend a Pro Arte http://www.proarte.co.uk Series 101 Prolene Watercolour Round (synthetic) size 16, widely available.

Cleaning—Hold under a cold tap at a downward angle and rotate 'throw' off the surplus water and place in a jar handle down. The brush should be symmetrical and pointed. If pigment remains, clean with baby shampoo. Do not squeeze brushes with a tissue or anything else. Stroking towards you on a kitchen towel will 'dry' the brush during painting.

Materials suppliers

The Wheatsheaf Art Shop 56 Baker Street, London W1M 1DJ
Tel: 020 7935 5284/5510 Wide range of materials. Good Catalogue.

The Art Shop 87 Bartholomew Street, Newbury, Berkshire, RG14 5EE
Tel: 01635 43171
http://www.artists-materials.co.uk/shop.html – currently Daler-Rowney offered online.

http://www.heatoncooper.co.uk/ online shopping (link on our peterturner.org web site) good site and service – no discounts offered – also see art-courses.org link.

http://www.jacksonsart.com – discounts offered see art-courses.org link.

Minerva Graphics 12A Trim Street, Bath Tel: 01225 464054

Tips—Watercolour

Composition—from life or photo look for what to simplify, loose, darken or to lighten and sometimes what to add (have a reference to hand). Start with a defined frame, without which overall composition is a lottery. Identify and mark ancor points.

Trees—branches and twigs should be thinner than those they came from, i.e. the further from the trunk the thinner. Many trees in the distance are a blur, with little colour or tone. Paint what you see not what you know.

Leaves—should be stippled or use a sponge (less controllable). Avoid brush stroke direction when 'stippling' leaves – simplify: Use two colours the lightest green and the darkest green in the tree. Make every use of the light and shade to improve body and shape.

People—in the middle distance – reduce shape, i.e. no arms or separate legs, sloping shoulders, taper to feet. Shadows are important. Make sure they are properly dressed.

Water—wash light distance to dark foreground, when dry keep ripples horizontal and smaller with distance, using the same colour and strength as the wash. Dab out Highlights and reflections (as in clouds and cross boarders between light and dark with horizontal ripples).

Clouds—wash with lightest cloud colour – often very dilute warm yellow – when dry wash blue from dark top to light bottom and quickly when still wet dab out clouds with folded kitchen roll. Observe back lit, top lit or side lit. Larger near, smaller with distance. Shadows in clouds are warm greys – very dilute.

Graduation—practise smooth graduations as in egg shells 'lift off' any sign of hard edges. Two or three light layers are more controllable than one dark layer.

APPENDIX W3 – Watercolour Continued

Paper stretching

Patient organised people stretch their paper before doing a painting. Less patient ones stretch when the painting is finished.

Materials—stout board, drawing board – may be home made from marine ply or better MDF and Butterfly (trade mark) Gumstrip sealing tape, gummed brown paper strip 35mm / 1 1/2" or better the 2" variety – available from most art and framing shops.

Soak the reverse of the painting/paper using a plastic water spray. Hold the paper over a sink, soak the paper again, the water will be dripping off the lower edge. Rotate the paper and let it drip off the top edge.

The paper will start to curl. Place, painting down, onto a dry draining board. Wait until the curl relaxes, by then it will be soaked through – 5 to 15 minutes depending on thickness of paper.

Place painting down onto the board and glue down each edge with the gum strip with equal width on the paper and the board. The gum strip should be very wet – use a 2" paint brush and water with one stroke.

Leave to dry naturally for 24 hours or until all is bone dry.

Cut the painting from the board with a craft knife and metal rule, just at the painting edge, using just enough pressure to cut only the gummed paper and not the board. The gummed paper stays on the painting which may now be framed.

Wet the gummed paper remaining on the board several times over a 15 to 30 minute period and pull it from the board.

Watercolour Shopping List:

Winsor & Newton ARTISTS' WATER COLOUR

Series / 5 or 14ml*

1 Winsor Yellow
   – Primary Yellow .... 1 / 14ml .... £_____
2 Yellow Ochre.................... 1 / 5ml .... £_____
3 Permanent Rose
   – Primary Magenta.................... 3 / 5ml .... £_____
4 Winsor Green
   (Yellow Shade).................... 1 / 5ml .... £_____
5 Winsor Blue
   (Green Shade)
   – Primary Cyan.................... 1 / 5ml .... £_____
6 Burnt Sienna.................... 1 / 5ml .... £_____
7 Neutral Tint (Black).................... 1 / 5ml .... £_____
8 Plastic 'Combination Palette' see photo .... £_____
9 Paper Arches not 300lb (640gsm) Qty 6 sheets
   cut to half or quarter size. .... £_____
10 Escoda: Kolinsky-Tajmyr Sable Round
   Watercolour Brush Series 1212 – Size 8.................... £_____
11 Pro Arte Series 101 Prolene Watercolour
   Round (synthetic) size 16.................... £_____
12 Pencil – Pentel P205 5mm clutch pencil .... £_____

13 Eraser – good quality soft maker? + Putty Rubber.................... £_____
14 Board, lightweight, (thick 1/8" plus) card or foam
   board, 2/3" larger than paper size, A3 is good for
   painting area up to 7" x 11". With 2 or 3
   bulldog clips .... £_____

TOTAL Watercolour .... £_____

Additional requirements for painting out of doors:

15 Stool or camping chair (aluminium is good)
   – Note: Arms get in the way.................... £_____
16 Second board or tray to place palette, water jar,
   paints, etc. on the ground (waterproof).................... £_____
17 Water carrier one to five litres.................... £_____
18 Kitchen role.................... £_____
19 Very large sun hat or sunshade, plus, factor
   20+ sun cream – very important, sunburn can
   ruin an out door painting experience.................... £_____

Notes. We do not recommend an easel for watercolour.
   *14 ml size tubes are more economic than 5ml. Buy
   two or three of the yellow.
   A pad of Langton's Watercolour paper is economic
   for test paper.

Figure W3

Recommended Palette Watercolour

Recommended Primaries Based Limited Palette:

Winsor & Newton Artists' Water Colours

Manufacturer's Recommendation	Fewer is better	5ml RR / Series	14ml RR / Series	Note:
1 Chinese White				Overkill
2 Winsor Lemon				Overkill
3 Winsor Yellow	1 Winsor Yellow			Yellow
4 Yellow Ochre	2 Yellow Ochre			
5 Scarlet Lake				Overkill
6 Permanent Rose	3 Permanent Rose			Magenta
7 Permanent Alizarin Crimson				Obsolete
8 Winsor Green (Blue Shade)	4 Winsor Green (Yellow Shade)			
9 French Ultramarine				Obsolete
10 Winsor Blue (Green Shade)	5 Winsor Blue (Green Shade)			Cyan
11 Burnt Sienna	6 Burnt Sienna			
12 Raw Umber				Neutral Tint
	7 Neutral Tint			Time saver

APPENDIX W4 – Watercolour Effects

Most common	
Leave – white paper	All highlights and white areas
Dab out – lift off before drying	Clouds, Reflections
Scratch	Highlights, repairs
Scrape	Highlights in water, various texture effects
Sponge, natural	Dab out and paint—bushes, leaves, textures
Eraser	Lighter tone—limited effect
Dab out – lift off after drying	Lighter tone—limited effect, also with damp cotton wool bud
Wash – after drying	Lighter tone—limited effect
Hard edge	Surrounds very wet area with jagged outline
Stipple	Leaves and various effects
Stipple – broken brush	As above cover more ground
Skim	Water ripples
Dry wash	Graduated skies and water
Wet wash	Solid non-graduated heavy light and heavy tone
Wet-in-wet	Various interesting effects with colour—not easily predictable
Questionable	
Masking Fluid – resist	Rarely needed—use throw away brush
Gouache	Not Watercolour
Plastic	In wet to make rocks—Random, Unreliable
Alcohol	Random, Unreliable
Granulation – sedimentary pigments	Unreliable
Wet area before wash	Unreliable, stimulates hard edge
Wax	Similar effect to Scraping—Unreliable, impossible to remove
Not Recommended	
Bleach	Bad reaction with paint and paper
Salt	Bad reaction with paint and paper

Exercise—Watercolour Palette Reference

The objective is to provide a reference to the colours and examples of the colours not included in the palette. It is also invaluable practise for mixing, tinting, shading and blending.

1. Paint each of the colours, as the reduced size 'map' below. Start with the light colours – bottom left going to top right, paint the full strength colour in the right hand 1/2 of the box, quickly (while the paint is still wet) – clean and dry the brush and 'move' some of the wet paint over the next 1/4 of the box, the paper will show through – clean the brush and start at the left with a very little clear water and let it merge – allow to dry. Do the same with all of the paints – do the yellow twice. If too liquid, graduation will be more difficult and the result not smooth.

2. Next practise mixing RGB colours:

Red – aim for a strong clear red as in a telephone box – mix on the palette mostly Winsor Yellow adding small amounts of Permanent Rose – then as above tint to White paper.

Green – mix mostly Yellow with small amounts of Winsor Blue – aim at a strong grass green.

Blue – Start with Permanent Rose and add small amounts of Winsor Blue. The blue should just loose its violet hue.

3. When dry, over-paint the Yellow Ochre in the 'Fix' box – the yellow in the centre should now be rich and dark, then paint a little less than the right-hand 1/4 of all the boxes with Neutral Tint (Black).

Apply the NT then quickly with a clean dry brush 'lift off' the left edge so that the blend is smooth.

Note: They all work well when NT is applied to a dark full strength colour. The shade from Black to Yellow and to a lesser extent any of the other colours which are not at full strength, is an unnatural cold harsh colour – this is the 'Shading Problem'. The solution, in the 'Fix' box, is to add a transition of Yellow Ochre between the Yellow and the NT.

Any cold harsh result can in most cases be solved by 'warming' the shade.

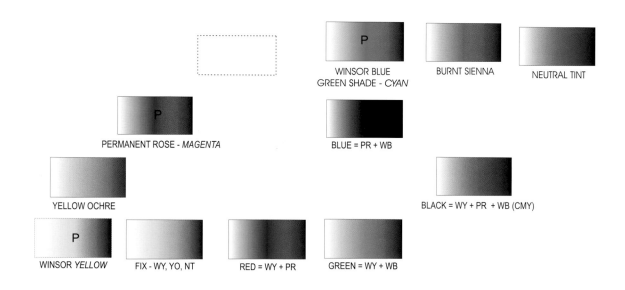

WINSOR BLUE GREEN SHADE - *CYAN* BURNT SIENNA NEUTRAL TINT

PERMANENT ROSE - *MAGENTA*

BLUE = PR + WB

YELLOW OCHRE

BLACK = WY + PR + WB (CMY)

WINSOR *YELLOW* FIX - WY, YO, NT RED = WY + PR GREEN = WY + WB

APPENDIX O1 – Oil

Care of materials
- Brushes – Squeeze out surplus paint with one or two layers of 'one time use' paper, phone books and Yellow Pages are ideal – Discard into cardboard carton
- Use 'turps' from the dipper to clean brushes during the painting – especially when a light colour is needed, use 2 / 4 layers of paper

Mixing
- Start with nearest colour
- More colours = more mud
- Mix of complementary colours, e.g. cyan and red, magenta and green, yellow and blue, all = black
- Use of black pigment is not recommended – makes colours 'dirty' or 'muddy' and used by itself creates 'black holes' in the painting

Drawing
Use an HB pencil, a single just visible line is best, avoid 'sketching'.

Economy
Take from tubes what you need when you need it   paint will harden in 1 to 14 days then is dead

Scale
Brush size large as possible but small enough for needed detail

Brushes, etc.
- Hog's Hair round No 2 – 5
- Hog's Hair flat No 8 – 12
- Sable or synthetic (Pro Arte 'Acrylix') – round No 2 – 6
- Double Dipper
- Disposable paper palette
- Canvas boards 10" x 12"
- Brush wash – W&N Distilled Turpentine – strong solvent – ventilate or W&N Sansodor low odour substitute
- Paint thinner – W&N Refined Linseed Oil – to replace lost support

Canvas
The Canvas Board is the most convenient and economical surface for oil painting. The stretched canvas, on a stretcher (with wedges), may be more acceptable if you are selling or exhibiting but is more expensive, and more difficult to handle and frame.

The surface is 'primed' for oil and acrylic use. With most boards these days made in China, expect varying quality and price.

Framing
Unlike watercolour where it is fashionable to minimise the impact of the frame on the painting with wide neutral mounts and simple neutral frames. Oil frames have no mounts or glass and are chosen to enhance the picture, the frame itself being much wider. Choosing a frame to enhance an oil painting is a specialised art in itself.

Standard Canvas Sizes

Inches	mm	Inches	mm	Inches	mm
7 x 5	177 x 127	14 x 10	356 x 254	20 x 16	508 x 406
10 x 8	254 x 203	18 x 14	457 x 356	22 x 18	558 x 457
12 x 10	305 x 254	20 x 16	508 x 406	24 x 18	610 x 457

Oil Painting Tips

Composition—from life or photo, look for what to loose and or simplify, to darken or lighten and sometimes what to add (have a reference to hand).

Trees—all branches and twigs should be thinner than those they came from, i.e. the further from the trunk the thinner they are.

Leaves—should be stippled. Avoid brush stroke direction when 'stippling' leaves. Observe the light and shade to improve body and shape.

Water—paint light distance to dark foreground, keep ripples horizontal and smaller with distance – use same colour with light above ripple and dark below. Cross edges of vertical reflections with horizontal ripples.

Clouds—keep all blues and whites separate. Start with lightest cloud colour – often White with a little Yellow Ochre. Observe back lit, top lit or side lit, larger near, smaller with distance. Shadows in clouds are warm greys, very little pigment is needed. Paint blue from dark top to light horizon. Very little blue dominates white.

People—in the middle distance – reduce shape make them slim, i.e. no arms or separate legs, sloping shoulders, taper to feet. Shadows are important. Make sure they are properly dressed.

Wet-in-Wet Oil Painting—is not helped much by smaller brushes. For hard fine edges—'push' the foreground or background paint to adjust the others edge or line. In wet-in-wet oils do not paint one colour or tone on top of another.

Recommended Palette Oil
Winsor and Newton ARTISTS' OIL COLOURS

Description
Artists Oil Colour 37ML TITANIUM WHITE
Artists Oil Colour 37ML WINSOR YELLOW - YELLOW
Artists Oil Colour 37ML YELLOW OCHRE
Artists Oil Colour 37ML WINSOR GREEN (YELLOW SHADE)
Artists Oil Colour 37ML PERMANENT ROSE - MAGENTA
Artists Oil Colour 37ML WINSOR BLUE (GREEN SHADE) - CYAN
Artists Oil Colour 37ML BURNT SIENNA
Artists Oil Colour 37ML RAW UMBER or CHARCOAL GREY

APPENDIX O2 – Oil Continued

Exercise—Oil Palette Reference

The objective is to provide a reference to the colours and examples of the key other colours not included in the palette. It is also useful practise for mixing, blending, tinting and shading.

Paint onto a half size board in the same locations as the palette paints each of the recommended colours in rectangles, as the reduced size 'map' below (without Winsor Green).

Start with the left hand 3rd of each rectangle which should be pure white, complete all 11. Use just enough paint to cover the area, if too much paint, blending will be more difficult.

The centre third of each rectangle should be pure paint just sufficient that the canvas does not show through.

Fill in a little less than the right hand third with Raw Umber or Charcoal Grey for all of the boxes.

Blend to achieve a smooth transition from white via each colour to black.

Note: They all work well except for the shade from Yellow to Black, which results in an unnatural harsh colour – this is to be avoided. The solution is to add a transition of warm dark Yellow between the Yellow and Black. In the rectangle next to the Yellow complete the blending from White via Yellow, dark Yellow (Yellow Ochre) and Black.

Next practise mixing the RGB colours:

Red – aim for a strong clear red as in the telephone box – mix on the palette mostly Winsor Yellow adding small amounts of Permanent Rose – then as above tint and shade.

Green – mix mostly Yellow with a small amounts of Winsor Blue – aim at a strong grass green.

Blue – Start with Permanent Rose and add small amounts of Winsor Blue. The blue should just loose its violet hue. To check the colour, mix a small amount with White elsewhere on the palette.

Oil Shopping List Oil:

Recommended Palette: Winsor & Newton ARTISTS' OIL COLOURS

Artists Oil Colour 37ML TITANIUM WHITE x2 .... £_____
Artists Oil Colour 37ML WINSOR YELLOW x2 .... £_____
Artists Oil Colour 37ML PERMANENT ROSE............................ £_____
Artists Oil Colour 37ML WINSOR BLUE
(GREEN SHADE) .... £_____
Artists Oil Colour 37ML BURNT SIENNA................................. £_____
Artists Oil Colour 37ML YELLOW OCHRE .... £_____
Artists Oil Colour 37ML RAW UMBER (BLACK)
OR CHARCOAL GREY... £_____
Artists Oil Colour 37ML WINSOR GREEN
(YELLOW SHADE)... £_____
A4 Disposable Palette – *see photo* .... £_____
Palette knife – *see photo*.._____
Oil Board 10" x 12" qty 6 .... £_____

Brushes:
1. Round Acrylix Synthetic size 2 .... £_____
2. Round Pro Arte B Hog size 3 .... £_____
3. Flat Hog no 8.. £_____

Pencil – Pentel P205 5mm clutch pencil .... £_____
Eraser – good quality soft – maker?..................................... £_____
Putty Rubber c 1.25 x 1.25" .... £_____
Double Dipper – *see photo* .... £_____
W&N Distilled Turpentine (brush wash) 75ml .... £_____
W&N Refined Linseed Oil
(only use to restore paint, *see page 52*) 75ml.................. £_____

.... TOTAL OIL £_____

WINSOR BLUE
GREEN SHADE - CYAN

BURNT SIENNA

RAW UMBER OR
CHARCOAL GREY

BLACK = WY + PR + WB (CMY)

PERMANENT ROSE - MAGENTA

RED = WY + PR

BLUE = PR + WB

GREEN = WY + WB

YELLOW OCHRE

WINSOR YELLOW

FIX - WY, YO, RU

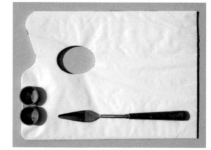

APPENDIX C – Colour

THE COLOUR WHEEL
—is a valuable aid to colour mixing. This is a small sample of the colours that the recommended primaries plus white are capable of.

Example: To make burnt sienna, start with yellow (Y) and add small amounts of Permanent Rose (M) until you reach Red (R) then add small amounts of Winsor Blue (C) until you arrive at burnt sienna.

Note: All opposites are complements, e.g. (C) and (R) complements mixed in the correct proportions equal black.

The colour wheel is also used, by designers, for what they call 'Colour Schemes'. These colour basics are valuable to all artists. See 'Colour Co-ordination' on page 30

THE CORRECT PRIMARY PIGMENTS

—are: Primary Cyan PB15:3, Primary Magenta PV19, Primary Yellow Py97.

Maimeri (Italy), Schmincke and Lukas are the only makers we are aware of in production of artists watercolour and oil paints labelled 'primaries':

E.G. Maimeri Blu: superior watercolours, Primary Blue – Cyan 400, Primary Red – Magenta 256, Primary Yellow 116

see http://www.maimeri.it/FineArts/colorprod.asp?mnu=0301

Oil Paints: Primary Cyan Classico 400 Primary Magenta Classico 256 Primary Yellow Classico 116

see http://www.maimeri.it/FineArts/colorprod.asp?mnu=0103.

For Acrylics Winsor & Newton Galeria and Daler-Rowney's System have 'Process' Red, Yellow and Blue as part of their range, these are also correct primaries.

Golden Fluid Acrylic includes the Primaries.

All of these makers are available from http://www.jacksonsart.co.uk

Index

Note: Table of Contents headings are not included in the index